Great Lakes Lighthouses

by Bruce Roberts and Ray Jones

SOUTHERN LIGHTHOUSES
Chesapeake Bay to the Gulf of Mexico

NORTHERN LIGHTHOUSES
New Brunswick to the Jersey Shore

WESTERN LIGHTHOUSES
Olympic Peninsula to San Diego

AMERICAN COUNTRY STORES

STEEL SHIPS AND IRON MEN
*A Tribute to World War II Fighting Ships
and the Men Who Served on Them*

GREAT LAKES LIGHTHOUSES

Ontario to Superior

Photographs by Bruce Roberts
Text by Ray Jones

A Voyager Book

The Globe Pequot Press

OLD SAYBROOK, CONNECTICUT

A Fresnel lens consists of separate, hand-polished prisms fitted into a metal frame. The prisms gather light, focusing it into a concentrated beam. Invented by French physicist Augustin Fresnel in 1822, a Fresnel would be manufactured in Paris, shipped across the Atlantic in pieces, and painstakingly reassembled inside a lantern room. Fresnels came in a variety of sizes, or "orders," ranging from sixth-order (about seventeen inches high and a foot wide) to first-order (as much as ten feet high and six feet wide). This third-order Fresnel still shines from the lantern room of the Point Gratiot lighthouse in Dunkirk, New York.

Copyright © 1994 by Bruce Roberts and Ray Jones

Library of Congress Cataloging-in-Publication Data

Roberts, Bruce.
    Great Lakes lighthouses : Ontario to Superior / photographs by Bruce Roberts; text by Ray Jones.
        p. cm.
    "A Voyager book."
    Includes bibliographical references and index.
    ISBN 1-56440-389-0
    1. Lighthouses—Great Lakes—History. 2. Great Lakes—History, Naval. I. Jones, Ray. II. Title.
VK1023.3. R63 1994
387.1' 55—dc20   93-45020
                                                 CIP

Cover photographs: Split Rock Light, Two Harbors, Minnesota; front, Cheryl Shelton-Roberts; back, Bruce Roberts
Book design by Nancy Freeborn

Printed in Hong Kong by Everbest Printing Co., Ltd. through Four Color Imports, Ltd.
First Edition / Second Printing

To Marion and Wes Roberts
—*Bruce Roberts*

Standing on the end of a long pier reaching out into Lake Michigan, the Frankfort Breakwater Light-house outshines a crescent moon.

ACKNOWLEDGMENTS

When my wife, Cheryl, and I started out photographing lighthouses on the Great Lakes, we had no idea how many people would help us along the way. Jeanne and George Couglar, caretakers at Tibbetts Point Light at Cape Vincent, New York, gave us the run of the place. Also, thanks goes to Shirley Hamblen, founder and past president of the Tibbetts Point Lighthouse Historical Society. Dick and Barb Lawson at Point Gratiot Lighthouse at Dunkirk, New York, came back at night so I could get the wonderful shot of the Fresnel lens on page iv; Marsha Hamilton at the State Historic Park at Mackinaw City, Michigan, dug out historical information about the lighthouse.

Lee Radzak, the site manager at Split Rock Lighthouse, put on his lighthouse keeper's uniform and turned on the big third-order Fresnel lens for my camera. Dick Moehl, president of the Great Lakes Lighthouse Keepers Association, and Jack Edwards, also of GLLKA, helped us get out to St. Helena Island to photograph the restored lighthouse. Don Terras of the Grosse Point Light in Evanston, Illinois, gave us his beautiful picture of the light at dusk. Dave Snyder, National Park Service historian of the Apostle Islands National Lakeshore, restored our faith in the national park system. Fran Platske, a lighthouse child who lived in the Apostles, gave us wonderful stories. Ken Black of the Shore Museum in Rockland, Maine, sent us photocopies of the Old Lighthouse Service bulletins. Gary Soule, curator of the Door County Maritime Museum in Sturgeon Bay, Wisconsin, provided information about the Door County lighthouses. Ann Hoge, a lighthouse keeper's daughter, sent us information on lighthouses from Copper Harbor to Passage Island, where she grew up. At Thirty Mile Lighthouse in New York, Thomas Harris loaned us his scrapbook. Wayne Wheeler and Marie Shaft at the United States Lighthouse Society shared information from the files in San Francisco.

Back in Washington, D.C., Dr. Robert M. Browning, historian of the United States Coast Guard, was there with a helping hand. Candace Clifford of the National Park Service Maritime Initiative compiled facts on American lighthouses. James Cassedy of the National Archives, Suitland Reference Division, found our lost notes and request for photocopies. James W. Claflin of Kenrick A. Claflin & Son, dealers in nautical antiques in Northborough, Massachusetts, took in earnest our requests for early lighthouse records.

And thanks to my wife, Cheryl, for putting up with long drives and late hours; for keeping notes that I would have lost; for carrying camera equipment up and down countless steps to lighthouses; and for smiles at the end of exhausting days.

—*Bruce Roberts*

Special thanks to Arthur Layton for his time and expertise in helping obtain information for the expansive area covered by this book. —*Ray Jones*

CONTENTS

Wearing a circa-1910 Lighthouse Service uniform, site manager Lee Radzak of the state-park system gazes out onto Lake Superior from the lantern room of Minnesota's famous Split Rock Lighthouse. No longer used as a navigational aid, the station's enormous clamshell lens once guided shipping through the world's largest freshwater lake. Today it inspires awe in thousands of summer visitors.

INTRODUCTION

Each November 10 Lee Radzak performs a ritual almost as old as civilization itself: lighting the lamp of a lighthouse. With darkness sweeping in from the east over the broad expanses of Lake Superior, Radzak sets about the evening chores that, in one form or another, have occupied lighthouse keepers since the time of the ancient Egyptians. Climbing the thirty-two-step spiral staircase of Minnesota's famed Split Rock Lighthouse, where he is resident keeper and historian, he checks the machinery. It all appears in proper working order. Laboriously, he raises the 250-pound weights that power the turn-of-the-century clockwork mechanism and rotate the light's heavy glass lens.

Radzak is meticulous in every detail of his task. He must take great care, partly because, for all its massiveness—the chandelierlike lens assembly weighs more than six tons—the operating parts of a lighthouse are quite delicate and easily damaged. But Radzak's precision reaches beyond mere prudence. It is, in fact, his way of honoring earlier Split Rock Lighthouse keepers, who took their work no less seriously than he.

Finally, Radzak throws the switch that brings the Split Rock Light to life. The big, French-made Fresnel lens brightens and begins to turn, flinging bright flashes out into the night at regularly spaced intervals. This is always a fine moment for Radzak, who takes pride in keeping alive an ages-old professional tradition.

For as long as ships have sailed the Earth's mighty lakes, seas, and oceans, men and women have struggled to keep lights burning on the shore and to guide mariners home from the deep. Throughout history sailors have anxiously scanned the dark horizon, searching for a light to help them find a safe harbor or avoid dangerous obstacles. Lake Superior's sailors, however, no longer look to Split Rock for guidance in the night. Its lighthouse has been blacked out on most nights since 1969, when the U.S. Coast Guard declared the light obsolete and put it out of service. Radio beacons, radar, and even satellites now do the work once done by the lighthouse and its keepers.

Coast Guard officials are anxious to keep the old lighthouse in the dark. During its annual ceremonial lightings, they require Radzak to limit its power sharply and adjust the beam of its huge lens out of focus with the horizon. Otherwise, seeing a light where there usually is none, the captains and navigators of ships out on the lake might be confused.

Although it serves no practical purpose, Radzak persists in firing up the Split Rock Lighthouse every November 10. The date is a significant one for him and for other lovers of lake lore and exciting sea stories. The lighting is a tribute to the brave captain and crew of the *Edmund Fitzgerald,* one of the most widely remembered ships ever to sail "the inland seas," also known as the Great Lakes. The ship and its crew of twenty-nine men met a tragic and mysterious end on November 10, 1975.

For as long as ships have sailed the seas, sailors nearing land have counted on shore lights to help them determine their positions, avoid dangerous obstacles, and find safe harbor. The earliest maritime peoples banked fires on hillsides to bring their sailors home from the sea. Occasionally, port cities and towns lacking suitable high ground for this purpose erected towers and placed a lamp or built a small fire at the top.

No one knows where the world's first true lighthouse was located, but the first one known to history served the Greco–Egyptian city of Alexandria. Soaring 450 feet into the sunny Mediterranean skies, it was also history's tallest lighthouse and the one with the longest service record. Built about 280 B.C. on an island called Pharos, inside the city's bustling harbor, it stood for more than a thousand years before being toppled by an earthquake near the end of the first millennium A.D. At night keepers lit a bright fire at the top of the huge tower to guide Phoenicians, Greeks, Carthaginians, Romans, and other mariners from all over the known world to this fabled and prosperous city. Most came to load their ships with grain from the Nile Delta. The rich soil of the delta was so wondrously productive that its grains fed Rome's legions and city dwellers all around the Mediterranean Basin and made possible the Roman Empire. But the grain would never have reached market without the ships that carried it and the lighthouse that guided their captains to port.

Like the Mediterranean of Roman times, North America's inland seas are today a heavily traveled commercial thoroughfare. Great Lakes freighters carry an endless variety of raw materials and finished products—iron ore to steel mills, metal parts to auto assembly plants, oil and chemicals to refineries, grain from the prodigious farms of the Midwest to hungry peoples all over the world.

The Great Lakes have been a key driving force in the American economy, and the long lake freighters and their brave crews have fueled that engine. But the prosperity brought by commerce has come at a high price: thousands of ships sunk and thousands of sailors drowned. The cost in vessels and lives would have been even higher if not for the lighthouses that ring each of the lakes.

For more than a century, lake sailors have been guided by a linked chain of navigational lights extending for more than a thousand miles from the St. Lawrence River to Duluth. Many of the lights, such those at Whitefish Point in Michigan and Charlotte in New York, have shined out over the lake waters since America itself was young. Most lake lighthouses are at least a century old, and all have played an essential role in the economic development and history of the United States and Canada.

THE SAGA OF THE *EDMUND FITZGERALD*

Anyone in America within hearing of a radio during the last decade is sure to have heard Gordon Lightfoot's "Ballad of the *Edmund Fitzgerald*." The song tells the true story of an enormous ship that sailed into the teeth of a prodigious storm on Lake Superior and, without warning or explanation, simply disappeared.

Most song lyrics worthy of serious attention have meaning on several levels, and this is certainly the case with Lightfoot's haunting ballad. But surely chief among its themes is that nature is unconquerable. The song reminds us that, even in this prideful technological age of instant satellite communication, radar navigation, and ships' bridges banked high with electronic hardware, human beings in general and sailors in particular are still at the mercy of the elements.

The incident described in the ballad took place only recently. This was no treasure ship wrecked along the Spanish Main four centuries ago, no early twentieth-century maritime disappearance attributed perhaps to latter-day pirates. No, Lightfoot's song is about a modern ship, a giant freighter 729 feet in length and displacing upward of 40,000 tons of water when fully loaded with iron ore. And the *Edmund Fitzgerald* vanished not from the mid-Pacific, the bowels of the Indian Ocean, or the storm-racked Caribbean but from the middle of a lake.

Here is the true story of the *Edmund Fitzgerald,* or as much of it as is known. When launched at River Rouge, Michigan, on a bright June day in 1958, she was the world's largest freshwater freighter. Named for a successful Milwaukee banker, she was as proud a ship as was ever lapped by lake water. Some called her "the Queen of the lakes," while others knew her as "the King." Her long, clean lines made her a fond and familiar sight to residents of port cities and towns from Toledo to Duluth. She became such a star that a Detroit newspaper ran a regular column to keep readers informed of her activities.

Indeed, the "Big Fitz" (the affectionate nickname used by her crew) was quite a ship. Able to carry more than 25,000 tons of iron ore, she had a muscular, 7,000-horsepower steam turbine that could whisk the big ship and her enormous cargo along at better than sixteen miles per hour. From 1958 onward, year after year, she set one record after another for carrying bulk freight. Usually the records she broke were her own. Her successes swelled the breasts of her captain and crew with pride and lined her owners' pockets with fat profits. By the time the *Edmund Fitzgerald* steamed out of Duluth, Minnesota, on the afternoon of Sunday, November 9, 1975, she had plied the shipping channels of the Great Lakes for more than seventeen years. She was still in her prime, by lake standards, and just as solid and capable as the day she was launched.

On this trip her holds were filled to the brim with 26,013 tons of taconite, marble-sized pellets of milled iron ore. Often she carried passengers as well as cargo and had two luxury staterooms and a comfortable lounge to accommodate them. But the Great Lakes are notorious for the great, dark, howling storms that churn their waters in the month of November. Potential lake passengers are wary of the month, as well they should be, and choose to travel shipboard earlier in the year. So the *Fitzgerald* left Duluth carrying only the taconite and twenty-nine lake sailors.

Most of the crew were midwesterners; fourteen of them were from Ohio and eight from Wisconsin. A few came from as far away as Florida or California. All were seasoned sailors, and older members of the crew especially had weathered many a raging Lake Superior gale. The men ranged from their midtwenties to near retirement age. At sixty-two Captain Ernest McSorley was among the oldest.

Signing on as a deck hand aboard a seagoing freighter at age eighteen, McSorley had made the merchant marine his livelihood and his life. Transferring to the lakes, the young sailor moved steadily up the chain of command, eventually becoming master of his own ship, the youngest master, in fact, on the Great Lakes. By November 1975 McSorley had been captain of the *Edmund Fitzgerald* for many years.

According to McSorley's friends the "Big Fitz" was, after his wife and family in Toledo, the love of his life. He rarely took time off, even when he was ill, and spent up to ten months a year aboard his ship. He knew her every quirk and idiosyncracy—her tendency to roll queasily or to bend and spring like a rebounding diving board in high waves. But McSorley had resolute faith in the ability of the *Fitzgerald* to weather a storm—even a Lake Superior storm in November. Perhaps that is why, when Monday, November 10 dawned, bringing gale warnings and fierce winds, McSorley kept the *Fitzgerald*'s bow pointed down-lake toward Whitefish Point and Sault Ste. Marie.

The *Arthur M. Anderson,* a U.S. Steel ore carrier under the command of Captain J. B. Cooper, had left Duluth not long after the *Fitzgerald.* When the weather turned unexpectedly sour, McSorley made radio contact with Cooper, whose ship trailed his own by about ten miles. The two captains agreed to stay in close communication and decided jointly that their ships would slip out of the traditional freighter channel along the lake's southern shores. Instead they would steer for the northeast, where the leeward shore might provide some protection from the weather. They would soon discover, however, that there was no shelter from this storm. By midday on the 10th, the *Fitzgerald* and *Anderson* were battling seventy-mile-per-hour winds and thirty-foot waves.

By the middle of the afternoon, the *Fitzgerald* had begun to show the beating she was taking. The force of the storm snapped the heavy cable fencing around the deck and washed it away. The ship took a more threatening blow when the waves smashed through a pair of ventilator covers. At about 3:30 P.M. Captain McSorley radioed the *Anderson* to report that he had water coming in. His vessel was operating at a list. Would the *Anderson* try to close the distance between the two ships? Yes, it would, came the reply.

Cooper had noticed no hint of desperation or even of serious concern in Captain McSorley's voice. In fact, the master of the *Fitzgerald* had given no indication at all, other than the damage reports and the request that the *Anderson* move in closer, that his ship was in trouble. Even so Cooper resolved to keep a close watch on the *Fitzgerald.*

The blasting wind and spray and the cloak of darkness that the storm had thrown over the lake made the huge ship invisible to the unassisted eye, but its enormous hull put a substantial blip on the *Anderson*'s radar screen. In the fury of this gale, however, even radar contact was tenuous. Occasionally, an eerie thing happened: When the towering waves swelled up to block the signal, the blip representing the *Fitzgerald* would flicker and disappear from the screen.

Despite the damage the *Fitzgerald* plowed steadily onward through the storm. Apparently, Captain McSorley was making for Whitefish Bay, where he hoped to find calmer waters. If he could round Whitefish Point and reach the bay, he might get his "Big Fitz" out of harm's way.

Since 1847 a lighthouse has stood on strategic Whitefish Point. In all the nearly 150 years since, rare has been the night when sailors on the lake could not count on its powerful light for guidance. But November 10, 1975, was just such a night. The early winter storm that had whipped Lake Superior into such a pitching cauldron had also vented its rage on the shore. It ripped down road signs, uprooted trees, and even bowled over a heavily loaded tractor-trailer on the Mackinac Bridge. Among the utility poles snapped in two by the high winds was one feeding electric power to the Whitefish Point Lighthouse. And so, ironically, on the night when the *Edmund Fitzgerald* needed it the most, there was no light at Whitefish Point.

Captain McSorley put out a call to all ships in his vicinity. Could anyone see the light at Whitefish Point? McSorley got an immediate reply from the Swedish freighter *Avafors* in Whitefish Bay. The pilot of the *Avafors* reported that neither the light nor the radio beacon at Whitefish Point was operating. The pilot inquired about conditions out on the lake.

"Big sea," said McSorley. "I've never seen anything like it in my life."

Still in the relative calm and safety of the bay, the *Avafors* had not yet borne the full brunt of the storm. But that was about to change. When they ventured beyond the lee of Whitefish Point and steamed out into the lake, the crew of the *Avafors* experienced McSorley's "big sea" for themselves. Mountainous waves pounded the hull of the saltwater freighter, and winds nearing hurricane force ripped across the deck. Eventually, the *Avafors* would win its battle with the lake. Not so the *Edmund Fitzgerald*.

As the storm raged on into the evening, Captain Cooper and the crew of the *Anderson* grew increasingly worried about their compatriots aboard the *Fitzgerald*. But there had been no "Mayday"—no call for help—from the "Big Fitz," only the damage reports.

An officer on the *Anderson* radioed the *Fitzgerald*. "How are you making out?" he asked.

"We are holding our own," came the reply. Those words were the last ever heard from the *Edmund Fitzgerald*.

The men on the bridge of the *Anderson* had grown used to the wavering, ghostly radar image of the *Fitzgerald*. The sea return, or radar interference caused by high waves, in this storm was tremendous. First the ship was there, then gone, then back again. Then, at some point shortly after 7:00 P.M. (no one aboard the *Anderson* ever knew exactly when), the *Edmund Fitzgerald* disappeared from the screen. And did not return.

Minutes passed. Officers on the *Anderson* bridge checked their radar equipment. There were other ships on the screen——upbound freighters struggling through the heavy weather. But there was no sign of the *Fitzgerald*. It was as if the giant ship, as long as a sixty-story building is tall, had slid down the side of a titanic wave and never come up again. Cooper ordered his men to try to take a visual sighting, but where the ship's running lights should have been there was only darkness. Frantic attempts to reach the *Fitzgerald* on radio were answered with silence.

Wasting no time, Captain Cooper put in a call to the Coast Guard. "No lights," he said. "Don't have her on radar. I know she's gone."

Here a blizzard has turned the Cleveland West Pierhead Lighthouse (1910) into a ghostly ice palace. Most lighthouses on the Great Lakes are shut down for several months every year while winter locks the lakes in its icy grip. (Courtesy U.S. Coast Guard)

At first Cooper's report of the disappearance was met with disbelief. How could a 729-foot-long freighter vanish, and in a matter of minutes? The skepticism of his Coast Guard radio contacts must have brought a sharp response from Cooper, who had had a harrowing day. Ships' captains are legendary for their mastery of certain forms of persuasive language. No doubt Captain Cooper said what was necessary to convince the Coast Guard.

A massive search and rescue operation swung into action. Despite the still savage weather, freshwater and saltwater freighters alike changed course and steamed toward the *Fitzgerald*'s last-known position. The captains and crews of these vessels were more than ready to put themselves at risk if there were any chance of saving fellow sailors perhaps even then tossing in the icy waves. Equally prepared to face the dangers of the storm were coastguardsmen, who rushed their fast cutters out onto the lake to join the search. Squadrons of aircraft, including huge C-130 transports and helicopters equipped with powerful search lights, crisscrossed the waters off Whitefish Point. But there was no sign of the *Fitzgerald*, nor of survivors. The Whitefish Point Lighthouse, which by now was back in operation, flung its light out over a Lake Superior seemingly empty of any trace of the *Edmund Fitzgerald*. Apparently, the lake had swallowed whole the ship, cargo, and crew.

As November 11 dawned the storm abated and skies began to clear. Searchers found scattered pieces of wreckage—a propane bottle, a wooden stool, a life vest, a lifesaving ring emblazoned with the letters FITZGERALD, but very little else. The shattered remains of a wooden lifeboat turned up later in the day, and with this discovery the chances of locating anyone alive among the *Fitzgerald*'s crew of twenty-nine dwindled to nothing. Actually, there had been scarce hope of finding survivors since midnight. The surface temperature of the lake was a numbing forty-nine degrees Fahrenheit. Anyone afloat in water that cold would likely go into shock within thirty minutes and would certainly be dead within four hours.

The search went on for days, but to little effect. By the end of the week, all the crew members of the ill-fated ship were pronounced officially dead. Family, close friends, and colleagues, who had already begun their grieving, gathered in homes and chapels in Toledo, Detroit, Duluth, and other towns and cities along the shores of the Great Lakes. Church bells rang twenty-nine times as the mourners paid tribute to memories of their friends, relatives, and lovers—but not to their earthly remains. None of the bodies was ever found.

What happened? What could cause a ship the size of the *Fitzgerald* to sink so suddenly and vanish so completely? After an official inquiry convened many months after the disaster, the Coast Guard pointed a collective finger of blame at the *Fitzgerald*'s hatch covers. If they were loose or had been damaged by the storm, the high waves washing over the deck might have poured through the hatches and flooded the cargo holds. At some point, having lost critical buoyancy, the big ship would have plunged to the bottom. Another theory put forward by several of McSorley's fellow freighter captains suggests that, perhaps unknowingly, he had grazed a shoal off Caribou Island. The damage caused by striking the shoal may have led to the flooding that took the *Fitzgerald* down. Probably the most popular theory concerning the wreck maintains that a pair of towering waves raised the bow and the stern of the ship simultaneously, leaving unsupported the long center section with its heavy cargo of iron ore. This might have caused the ship to snap in two, with the stern section rapidly following the bow to the bottom. But of course no one will ever know for sure what killed the *Fitzgerald* or what took place during those crucial moments before she went down. There were no witnesses left alive to tell the tale. According to a legend of the Ojibwa Indians, a people who have lived by the lakes for longer than even they can remember, the big lake we call Superior "never gives up the dead."

That the Ojibwa have such a legend is proof enough that they and other native peoples often ventured out onto the Great Lakes in their long canoes to fish, to trade, and to travel. No doubt they suffered calamitous wrecks of their own. The stories of those adventures, some of them tragedies, are lost in the mists of time. Or, like that of the *Edmund Fitzgerald*, they are locked away in a ghostly chamber of ice-cold water at the bottom of a lake.

Lighthouses (like the Michigan City East Pier Light, above) became the subject of one of the very first acts of Congress in 1789 when responsibility for construction and operation of coastal lights was placed in the hands of the Treasury Department. Alexander Hamilton, whose face stares out at us from the $10 bill, became the first head of the Lighthouse Service. Among Hamilton's successors was Stephen Pleasonton, a Treasury auditor who presided over the service like an oriental satrap for nearly half a century. Pleasonton's tight-fisted stodginess delayed introduction of the advanced Fresnel lens for decades. A Lighthouse Board composed of engineers and maritime professionals replaced Pleasonton in 1852, making rapid improvements in America's growing list of navigational lights. The board promoted widespread use of the powerful Frenchmade Fresnels. From 1910 until 1939 the Service was governed by a separate government Bureau of Lighthouses. Then, just before World War II, responsibility for lighthouses and other navigational markers was placed entirely in the hands of the U. S. Coast Guard. Since that time, many lighthouses have been discontinued and all but one (the Boston Harbor Lighthouse) have been automated. Sadly, lighthouse keepers are now an extinct professional species in America.

CHAPTER ONE

LIGHTS OF
THE GATEWAY LAKE

Ontario

Tibbetts Point Lighthouse graces the horizon of a New York sunset.

Lights of the Gateway Lake

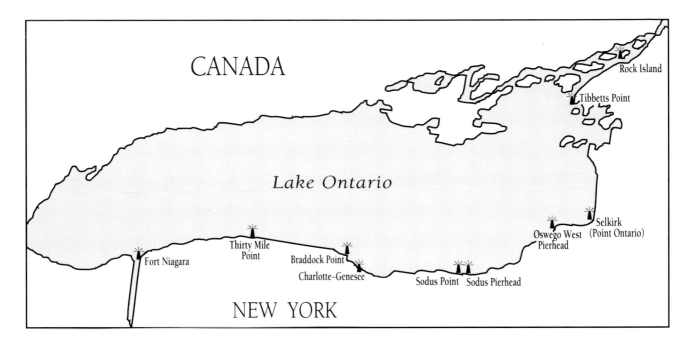

CANADA

Lake Ontario

NEW YORK

Rock Island

Tibbetts Point

Selkirk
(Point Ontario)

Oswego West
Pierhead

Thirty Mile
Point

Fort Niagara

Braddock Point

Charlotte–Genesee

Sodus Point   Sodus Pierhead

A freshwater inland sea, Lake Ontario attracts plenty of gulls—not to mention ships, which need navigational lights to guide them safely to port. Just off New York's Sodus Point, the lighthouse above stands at the end of a lengthy pier, an arrangement characteristic of many Great Lakes lighthouses.

L ighthouses are among the most prominent and recognizable manmade structures on the planet. Precisely because of their status as navigational markers, they are closely identified with certain geographic or natural features. For instance, it is difficult to think of Minnesota's Split Rock as separate from the Split Rock Lighthouse. Lighthouse towers almost seem the products of nature, as if they had been carved from native stone and left behind by the retreating glaciers of the last ice age. Of course, the Great Lakes themselves, which provide the reason for most of America's inland lighthouses, were in fact created by this chiseling action of ice and water on stone.

Each of the Earth's continents has at least one natural feature that stands out in our minds as a symbol for all its diverse lands and peoples. For Africa that feature is probably the Nile; for Asia, Mount Everest; for Australia, Ayers Rock; for South America, the Amazon; for Europe, the Alps or perhaps the Greek Isles. But since most of us reading this book live in North America and have differing regional loyalties, the selection of such a symbol for this continent may seem a little more difficult. For instance, some might put forward the Mississippi River, while others may suggest Mount McKinley, the Colorado Rockies, or the California redwoods. Upon reflection, however, the available choices can easily be reduced to one.

A few miles from the city of Buffalo, New York, is a natural phenomenon so majestic and so powerful that every year it strikes millions of people speechless with awe. Tourists flock to see it from every state in the Union, every Canadian province, and, literally, every nation on earth. Children the world over have heard of this place and, no doubt, dreamed of traveling to America to enjoy it for themselves. The phenomenon in question is, of course, Niagara Falls.

Actually a pair of falls, the American and Horseshoe, one on either side of the U.S./Canadian border, they form what is arguably the world's most popular and most visited natural wonder. And why not? Fed by the overflow from four of the earth's largest lakes, the falls are very impressive indeed. More than 40 million gallons of water plunge over them every minute. This unforgettable display of nature's raw power has inspired poets, politicians, and countless ordinary people, not to mention generations of young couples who have flocked to the falls, to celebrate, and consummate, their marriages.

MARRIAGE OF WATERS

Why do the Niagara Falls exert such a pull on us? Maybe it is because they help us understand our place in the natural scheme of things. Certainly, the falls are a key to understanding the Great Lakes and the leviathan geological forces that created them. Hundreds of millions of years ago, this region was covered by a warm, shallow sea teeming with life. Along the margins of the sea, colonies of tiny, shelled creatures piling one atop the other over millions of years built up an immense barrier reef. Eventually, the land was uplifted, the seas drained, and the ancient reef compacted into tough limestone.

Several times during the past million years, great sheets of ice, up to two miles thick, have pushed across the northern half of our continent. Like frozen bulldozers with blades a thousand miles wide, they scooped out basins. When the ice melted it filled the basins with water, forming lakes. But the stubborn limestone had resisted the ice and remained behind as a natural dike at the eastern end of Lake Erie. Today the waters of Erie, Huron, Michigan, and Superior spill over the dike, dropping several hundred feet in just a few miles on the way to Lake Ontario. The most dramatic descent is, of course, at Niagara, where the blue lake water plunges 184 feet over American Falls and 176 feet over Horseshoe Falls.

THE BEAVER CONNECTION

Among the very first Europeans to see the falls was Samuel de Champlain, father of New France and founder of the city of Quebec. Champlain pushed up the St. Lawrence River, explored Lake Ontario, and may have reached Niagara as early as 1604, several years before the English established their first colony in Virginia at Jamestown. No doubt the majesty of the falls impressed Champlain, but the French adventurer had much more to awe him besides: an entire pristine and unexplored new world. The Huron Indians told Champlain that beyond the falls lay several lakes even bigger than Ontario and a vast, wild region rich in furs and minerals. Initially, Champlain may have doubted their stories, but he and other astonished French explorers would soon learn they were true. The falls were fed by an enormous system of swift-running rivers and huge lakes, reaching back a thousand miles or more into the very heartland of the North American continent. The French quickly saw the potential of all these interconnected waterways—they could be used as a convenient and highly profitable commercial highway.

It has been said that, more than any human adventurer, the humble beaver deserves credit for opening up the North American interior. Much prized by hatmakers and the fashion-conscious ladies and gentlemen of Europe, beaver pelts gave tough French trappers a cash incentive for exploring America. Following every river and stream all the way to its source, they loaded sturdy bark canoes with pelts and then paddled and portaged them eastward along at least part of what is known today as the St. Lawrence Seaway.

It may be that the French built signal fires or placed lanterns on poles to guide their canoe freighters to key portages, villages, and fur-trading centers. It was the British, however, who would build the first true lighthouse on the Great Lakes.

For more than 150 years, the British wrestled with the French for control of the lakes and the access they provided to the interior of the continent. This struggle reached its climax in 1759, during the French and Indian War, when an army of redcoats, under the command of General James Wolfe, appeared outside the city walls of Quebec. The Marquis de Montcalm rushed out from behind the walls at the head of a poorly trained force of irregulars to confront Wolfe and was promptly defeated. Although both commanders were killed, the battle ended in near total defeat for the French. Having captured Quebec, the city of Champlain, the British took possession of Canada and the strategic Great Lakes waterways. But complete British dominion over the lakes would be short-lived.

REVOLUTIONARY GHOST SHIP

Only fifteen years after their victory over the French, the British found themselves once more at war in America. This time the fight was against their own unruly colonists. During this Revolutionary War the British maintained a powerful navy on the Great Lakes. Among their most formidable lake warships was HMS *Ontario*. Launched during the late spring of 1780, she was at least eighty-feet long and square-rigged like an oceangoing fighting ship. Armed with sixteen six-pound cannon and six four-pounders, she had more than enough firepower to crush any American vessel that might challenge her mastery of Lake Ontario. The weather and the lake itself, however, could not be fought with cannon shot and gunpowder. The *Ontario* was destined to lose its only battle—with one of the Great Lakes' notorious autumn storms.

Late in October 1780 the *Ontario* weighed anchor and set sail from Niagara, bound for Oswego, New York, with a load of British soldiers, military supplies, and an army payroll chest brimming with gold and silver coins. On Halloween a gale came whistling out of the west, and by the time it had blown itself out the following morning, the *Ontario* was gone. Vanishing along with it were four women, five children, several Indians, and more than seventy soldiers and seamen. As with the *Edmund Fitzgerald* and so many other disappearances on the Great Lakes, this one remains a mystery to this day. Poignantly, settlers found dozens of British Army caps bobbing in the waves along the south shore of the lake; but there were no other clues to the fate of the ship or its passengers, crew, and cargo. Treasure hunters, interested in valuable relics—not to mention the payroll chest—have searched endlessly for the wreck. Most believe the *Ontario* met its end near Thirty Mile Point. The discovery in 1954 of a very old anchor not far from the point lends weight to this opinion, but the ship itself has never been found.

Ironically, countless sailors may owe their lives indirectly to the sinking of the *Ontario*. The loss of this fine ship alerted British authorities to the need for better navigation markers on the Great Lakes. In 1781, the year after the *Ontario* disaster, they placed a light, fueled by whale oil, on the roof of Fort Niagara, at the mouth of the Niagara River. The French had built the old stone fortress in 1726 to help protect fur traders portaging their pelts from the upper lakes. The British had taken control of the fort after the French and Indian War. The fort and its light, the first established on the Great Lakes, became the property of the United States following the Revolutionary War.

ROCK ISLAND LIGHT

Rock Island, New York – 1847 and 1882

To reach the Great Lakes from the ocean, ships must push several hundred miles up the ever-narrowing St. Lawrence River. Toward the end of this river journey are the Thousand Islands, which guard the approaches to Lake Ontario. Six lighthouses were built along the river and among the islands to guide ships and warn them of obstacles. One of the best preserved of these is the Rock Island Lighthouse, established in 1847 and rebuilt in 1882.

The Rock Island Lighthouse has its feet in the river. Built just off the island on a concrete foundation, the forty-foot, conical limestone tower is connected to land by a stone walkway. The lantern once held a sixth-order Fresnel lens, but following World War II, the station was deactivated and the old lens removed. At one time the lamps were powered by a gasoline generator located in a separate structure near the dwelling. Active for almost a century, the light has served countless thousands of vessels steaming along the St. Lawrence, going to and from the Great Lakes.

Rock Island Lighthouse is reachable by the water only. (Courtesy U.S. Coast Guard)

Rock Island is accessible only from the water, and while no public transportation to the island is available, private boats may stop here. The lighthouse is usually open to the public from 8:00 A.M. to 4:30 P.M. during the summer months, but it is best to make sure by calling ahead. For information call (315) 654–2522. The lighthouse can also be seen from Thousand Island Park, on Wellesley Island; and from the community of Fisher's Landing, off Route 12 at Route 180, just a few miles southwest of the Thousand Island Bridge. For information on events and facilities in the Thousand Islands region, write the Thousand Islands International Council, Box 400, Alexandria Bay, New York 13607 or call (800) 8–ISLAND.

TIBBETTS POINT LIGHT
Cape Vincent, New York – 1827 and 1854

Lighthouses are nearly always strategically located, but that is especially true of Tibbetts Point Lighthouse in Cape Vincent, New York. Its light marks the entrance to the St. Lawrence River and the beginning of the last leg of any journey from the Great Lakes to the Atlantic. Recognizing the importance of the place to commercial shipping, the government placed a light station here in 1827. The stone tower stood fifty-nine feet high and employed a whale-oil lamp and reflector lighting system.

Countless vessels bound from Lake Ontario to the Atlantic Ocean have passed by the sixty-nine foot tower of Tibbetts Point Lighthouse. Since 1854 the stucco structure has stood the test of wind, weather, and time.

The sun drops into Lake Ontario behind the tower of Tibbetts Point Lighthouse. Located where Ontario's waters flow into the St. Lawrence River, the lighthouse marks the eastern limits of the Great Lakes region. Not surprisingly, this is an excellent place for early evening photography.

The light tower that can be seen at Cape Vincent today replaced the earlier lighthouse in 1854. Its sixty-nine-foot stucco tower was given a fourth-order Fresnel lens lighted by a fifty-candlepower oil lamp. A steam-powered fog signal began operation in 1896. The station was automated by the Coast Guard in 1981.

Cape Vincent has spectacular sunsets, and the lighthouse grounds offer an excellent place to view and photograph them. Nearby are several historic islands, including Wolfe Island, named for the British general who captured Quebec, and Carelton Island, a frequent gathering place for large Mohawk war parties.

To reach the lighthouse from Cape Vincent and New York Highway 12E, follow Lighthouse Road for 2½ miles to the cape. The grounds are open daily for walking, picnicking, and photography. The keeper's house now serves as an American Youth Hostel, open from May 15 to October 15. For hostel reservations call (315) 654–3450. This is a gorgeous place for sunset photographs.

SELKIRK (PORT ONTARIO) LIGHT
Selkirk (Pulaski), New York – 1838

Although its beacon served lake sailors for little more than twenty years, the Selkirk Lighthouse is one of the more fascinating and historic buildings on the Great Lakes. Built in 1838, it was taken out of service in 1859, when the local fishing and shipbuilding industries began to fade. Fortunately, the old lighthouse has survived. Its gabled fieldstone dwelling and old-style lantern are o. considerable architectural and historical interest.

Light glows warmly from Selkirk's lantern and keeper's dwelling, now a rustic hostelry frequented by salmon fishermen.

The first settlers came to Port Ontario to harvest the Atlantic salmon that came here in prodigious numbers to spawn. The fishermen were followed by sailors and shipbuilders, who built homes beside the lake and along the banks of the appropriately named Salmon River. In one way or another, most of the men in the area relied for their living on Lake Ontario. With its dangerous, unpredictable weather, the lake was a fickle and sometimes death-dealing friend. That is why, according to legend, houses hereabouts have an unusually large number of windows, for the wives of fishermen and sailors kept a constant eye on the lake for some sign of their menfolk.

The Selkirk Lighthouse also has its share of windows. Built for $3,000 by local contractors with stone quarried nearby, the old dwelling is one of a kind. The small lantern room projecting through the roof is also highly unusual. It is of an early type in use before Fresnel lenses became common (about the middle of the nineteenth century). Originally, the lantern held fourteen-inch parabolic reflectors and eight mineral-oil lamps. The light could be seen from about fourteen miles out on the lake. Shortly before the lighthouse was discontinued, the outdated reflector system was replaced by a sixth-order Fresnel lens.

When the Salmon River began to silt up and ship traffic dropped off, the government saw little need for a light here. The building was eventually sold for use as a private residence and then as a hotel. Although its lantern was dark for more than 130 years, the old lighthouse is now back in operation. In 1989 the owners received permission from the Coast Guard to place an automated light in the lantern. The light is designated a Class 11 navigational aid.

The lighthouse is privately owned and not open to the public. It can, however, be seen from the road. Take Route 3, which parallels the lakeshore a few miles west of I–81, to Port Ontario and turn onto Lake Road. The lighthouse stands at the end of the road, at the mouth of the Salmon River. The old stone lighthouse is being restored by the owners who rent it for overnight accommodation. Here's a wonderful chance to spend the night in a real lighthouse. For information call (315) 298–6688. This area is very popular with fishermen, who flock here when the salmon are running.

OSWEGO WEST PIERHEAD LIGHT
Oswego, New York – 1822, 1836, and 1934

Over the course of nearly one and three-quarters centuries, at least three different lighthouses have served the port city of Oswego, guiding vessels in and out of its bustling harbor. The first, a simple stone tower and keeper's dwelling built in 1822, stood at Fort Ontario on the east bank of the Oswego River.

As shipping on Lake Ontario increased and Oswego grew into an important commercial center, the need for a better, more powerful light became apparent. In 1836 a fine new lighthouse was built, at the end of a long pier on the west side of the harbor. An octagonal gray tower with attached oil room, it boasted a third-order Fresnel lens displaying a fixed white light that could be seen from fifteen miles out

The busy port city of Oswego has been served by several lighthouses, the earliest built in 1822. The Oswego West Pierhead Lighthouse shown above was placed in service in 1934. Still in operation, it displays a red flashing light. Notice the twin antenna masts of the station's radio beacon.

on the lake. Tended by several generations of keepers, the light burned for almost a century. The hearts of Ontario's sailors and Oswego old-timers were saddened when the wrecking crews pulled down the old tower in 1930.

The government had no intention of leaving Oswego's harbor unmarked for long, however, and plans were already in the making for a third lighthouse. By 1934 it was in service. Consisting of a relatively short metal tower and a small attached dwelling, each with white walls and a red roof, the lighthouse stands on a concrete pier at the end of a long stone breakwater. Fitted with a rotating, fourth-order Fresnel lens, the lantern displays a flashing red light. Tinted window panels in the lantern give the light its characteristic color.

In 1942 several men drowned only a short distance from the lighthouse, during what was to have been a routine exchange of keepers. Not long afterward Coast Guard officials decided to automate the light.

Another historic Oswego attraction is Fort Ontario. Built as a frontier bastion by the British in 1755, during the French and Indian War, Fort Ontario fell to the forces of the Marquis de Montcalm in 1756. The French destroyed the fort before retreating toward Quebec, where they themselves were eventually defeated. The British rebuilt the fortress, only to see it overrun by an army of American revolutionaries in 1778. During the War of 1812, the British returned to bombard and overwhelm the fort. The undermanned defenders had only six cannon, which were in such bad shape that they had been condemned. Fort Ontario also saw service in the Civil War and in World War II, when it was used as a refugee center.

Although the lighthouse itself is off limits to the public, it can be seen and enjoyed from several vantage points in Oswego. The best is probably Bretbeck Park. From Route 104 turn toward the lake on West First Street. Turn left on Van Buren and then right on Lake Street. The park is just beyond Wright's Landing.

While in the area you may want to visit Oswego's H. White Marine Museum or the locks of the historic Oswego Canal. Also nearby is Fort Ontario, where you can see the keeper's residence of the original Oswego Lighthouse.

SODUS POINT LIGHT

Sodus Point, New York – 1825 and 1871

On June 19, 1813, the citizens of sleepy Sodus Point, New York, had an uncharacteristically noisy day. A British fleet had sailed across Lake Ontario and rudely awakened them with cannon fire. The British fleet landed troops, but the redcoats were stopped and eventually driven off by a hastily gathered force of militia. To raise the alarm a local horseman rode, Paul Revere–style, through the countryside to warn farms and villages that "the British are coming."

From 1825 until just after the turn of the century, Sodus Point Lighthouse offered mariners a different sort of warning: its bright beacon, announcing clearly that land was near. Unexpected encounters with land are nearly always fatal to ships and all too often to their crews as well. Ship captains and residents in this area had petitioned Congress for a light to guide sailors safely into Sodus Bay. Eventually, they were rewarded by construction of a rough split-stone tower and dwelling.

Completed during the administration of President John Quincy Adams, these structures remained in use for more than forty years. Following the Civil War they

A grand survivor from an earlier time, the 1871 Sodus Point Lighthouse still stands at lake's edge. The light in the lantern room was extinguished in 1901 when the nearby pierhead lighthouse (on page 24) took over its duties. Today, the venerable structure houses a maritime museum. Its tower offers visitors a fine view of Lake Ontario.

fell into a sad state of disrepair, and the government replaced them with a forty-five-foot-high, square stone tower and an attached two-story dwelling. The light has been inactive since 1901, its job taken over by a nearby pier light.

Today the station structures are maintained by the Sodus Bay Historical Society. The dwelling now contains a delightful maritime museum. Visitors will want to see the 3.5-order Fresnel lens in the tower.

Looking something like a chess rook, the Sodus Point Pierhead Lighthouse still guides lake shipping. It stands at the end of a long concrete pier connecting it to the mainland. This makes the light easier to see from the water and, so, more useful to navigators.

To reach the Old Sodus Lighthouse, take Route 104, turn north on Route 14 into the village of Sodus Point, then left onto Ontario Street (at the firehall). The lighthouse is open weekends from July to mid-October, but hours may vary. For information call (315) 483–4936. The tower can be climbed for a close-up look at the old Fresnel lens and a spectacular view of Sodus Bay and the lake beyond.

CHARLOTTE–GENESEE LIGHT

Rochester, New York – 1822

The Charlotte-Genesee Lighthouse was not built until well after the War of 1812. Had it been built earlier, it might have become the target of British cannon. During that war the British made repeated visits to the mouth of the Genesee River, blasting away at homes and businesses with heavy cannon. The redcoats never mounted a full-scale invasion of the place, however, perhaps because residents were always prepared to take up arms against them. Cannon balls fired by the British became prizes of local residents. Some were actually used for industrial purposes, such as crushing stone and grinding indigo.

Completed in 1822 at a cost of $3,301 and dropped from active service in 1881, Genesee Light is now the second-oldest lighthouse on the Great Lakes. The grand old lighthouse owes its existence in part to students of nearby Charlotte High School, who have made it their symbol. In 1965, when it was rumored that the lighthouse would be torn down, students at the school began a successful campaign to save the structure. Responding to student petitions and other public pressure, the government handed the lighthouse over to the Charlotte–Genesee Lighthouse Historical Society. The station has now been restored, and its museum is operated under a permanent charter from New York State. The Coast Guard contributed a Fresnel lens from its Cleveland (Ohio) station to the restoration effort.

The stone tower and brick dwelling at Charlotte-Genesee Lighthouse are two of the Great Lakes' most historical structures.

More than 170 years ago, the forty-foot-high octagonal limestone tower was erected on the edge of a bluff overlooking the mouth of the Genesee River and Lake Ontario beyond. David Denman, the station's first keeper, lived beside the tower in a rustic, two-room limestone cottage. Each night Denman trudged up the tower steps to light the ten Argand lamps that produced the light concentrated by a set of reflectors. These relatively inefficient reflectors were exchanged for a fourth-order Fresnel lens in 1852. The current two-and-a-half-story brick dwelling replaced the cottage in 1863.

As part of renovations at the Genesee light station, government crews built a pier, placing a second small lighthouse tower at the end. In 1853 an August northeaster sent waves crashing over the pier, making it extremely difficult for keeper Samuel Phillips to reach the tower on the pier and fire up the lamp there. Former lighthouse

keeper Cuyler Cook happened to be nearby with a boat and offered to row Phillips out to the tower. Cook paid for this generosity with his life. While Phillips was tending the lamp, the waves swamped Cook's boat and drowned him.

In 1884 lighthouse officials decided to move the primary light station's apparatus to the pier and abandon the original lighthouse. Luckily, the old octagonal tower survived a century of disuse and remains today a reminder of an earlier, more romantic era. In 1974 the Genesee Lighthouse was placed on the National Register of Historic Places.

Visible through a narrow passageway, a spiral staircase leads upward to the lantern room atop the tower. As the date over the door confirms, the rough stone tower has stood since 1822.

From the east take the Seaway Trail (Lakeshore Boulevard), then follow Lake Avenue north to Holy Cross Church. From the west of Rochester, take Lake Ontario State Parkway to Lake Avenue. The lighthouse and its parking lot are located behind the church. The lighthouse complex is now leased to the Charlotte–Genesee Lighthouse Historical Society, which opens the tower and dwelling to the public on weekends. The grounds are open daily. Special tours are available by appointment. For information phone (716) 621–6179.

BRADDOCK POINT LIGHT

Hilton, New York – 1896

For more than fifty-seven years, the Braddock Point Lighthouse tower stood proud and tall, marking the western approaches to the city of Rochester, New York. Focused by a 3.5-order lens, its 20,000-candlepower light was among the brightest on the Great Lakes. Ships' captains reported seeing the light from more than eighteen miles out on Lake Ontario.

The extraordinary tower was also one of the lake's most distinctive daymarks. Built during the mid-1890s, at the height of the Victorian era, it featured a decorative gallery and peaked roof suggestive of the elaborate helmet of a European calvary officer.

Unfortunately, the old lighthouse weathered one too many of Lake Ontario's prodigious storms. By 1954 the structure had suffered damage so extensive that the building itself became a safety hazard. The Coast Guard had no choice but to extinguish the light and pull down the top two-thirds of the tower, to keep it from falling under its own weight.

Today the Braddock Point Lighthouse, with its squat, truncated tower, is a private residence and not open to the public. It can be viewed from the road, although visitors are warned to keep off the property.

Braddock Point Lighthouse was eminently more photogenic before its unfortunate decapitation in 1954. (Courtesy National Archives)

The lighthouse is located at the end of Lighthouse Road, just off the Lake Ontario State Parkway and west of Braddock Bay. The old lighthouse can be viewed from the road; however, visitors are reminded not to trespass on this property, as it is privately owned.

THIRTY MILE POINT LIGHT

Somerset, New York – 1876

Located on a point of land thirty miles east of the mouth of the Niagara River, the square stone tower of Thirty Mile Point Lighthouse rises seventy-eight feet above the level of Lake Ontario. The scenic point on which the lighthouse stands is memorable, not only because it is a convenient mile marker but also because of the waves of history that have washed over this place.

In 1678 a twenty-ton sailing vessel under the command of the French explorer La Salle was wrecked off the point. A century later, during the Revolutionary War, the British fighting ship HMS *Ontario* was believed to have gone down near Thirty Mile Point, with the loss of eighty-eight lives. A two-master armed with heavy cannon, the *Ontario* was carrying British troops for duty against continental forces in

Thirty Mile Point Lighthouse offers visitors a self-guided tour. A nature trail leads from the grounds into Golden Hill State Park.

New York as well as an Army payroll estimated at $15,000, when she foundered during a blizzard. Divers believe the wreck lies on the lake bottom only a mile or two off Thirty Mile Point. In 1954 an anchor believed to be from the *Ontario* was recovered off the point and is displayed at the Fort Ontario Museum.

Some say Golden Hill takes its name from the glittering Army payroll supposedly washed or brought ashore from the wreck. There have been no few unsuccessful attempts to dig up the treasure. A less dramatic explanation for the name, which has the support of local historians, is the profusion of goldenrod that once bloomed on an island off the point. The island has been eroded away along with the dangerous sandbar that once lay off the point. Yet rumors of buried treasure at Golden Hill persist.

As long ago as 1834, a local farmer told his neighbors of being startled by a group of men who had rowed up Golden Hill Creek to dig up a chest from the creek bank. He said they took the chest back to a waiting schooner. Similar stories were probably told during the Prohibition era of this century. It is said that smugglers often brought illicit shipments of liquor ashore here.

The Thirty Mile Point Lighthouse was built on Golden Hill in 1875, at a cost of $90,000. It remained in service until 1959, when the light was automated and transferred to a slender steel tower nearby. The gray square-cut stones of the original tower were shipped from Chaumont Bay near the St. Lawrence River and then hauled up the steep banks of Golden Hill.

A Fresnel lens manufactured in France was installed in the eight-foot-diameter lantern room. The handmade French lens concentrated the light produced by a kerosene flame to a strength of 600,000 candlepower. Sailors could see the light from up to eighteen miles away. In 1885 the kerosene flame was replaced with one of the earliest electric bulbs ever placed in a lighthouse. The light produced by the combination of the old Fresnel lens and Mr. Thomas Edison's newfangled invention became the strongest on Lake Ontario and the fourth strongest in the Great Lakes.

Today the Thirty Mile Point Lighthouse is one of the main attractions of Golden Hill State Park. The park offers campsites, picnic tables, a marina, and an engaging nature trial. Visitors can also take a self-guided tour of the lighthouse. From Route 18 drive north on Route 269 and then west on Lower Lake Road. For more information, call Golden Hill State Park at (716) 795–3885.

FORT NIAGARA LIGHT
Youngstown, New York – 1781, 1823, and 1872

Located at Youngstown, New York, at the juncture of the Niagara River and Lake Ontario, Fort Niagara Lighthouse stands as a mute reminder of early struggles for economic and political dominance in North America. Now an automated light station, the stone building attached to the tower is leased from the Coast Guard by the Old Fort Niagara Association, which uses it as a museum and gift shop.

By the late seventeenth century, the Niagara River and its portages around Niagara Falls, which connect Lake Ontario to Lake Erie and the upper Great Lakes, had become important to French fur traders as they ventured ever deeper into the continent's interior. In 1726 the French built Fort Niagara, which came to be known as the "French Castle." The French maintained a few sailing vessels on Lake Ontario, but canoes and bateaux were the principal means of hauling freight and passengers. The French fort acted as a large daymark for these small vessels. They also followed the plume of vapor rising from Niagara Falls; the plume could be seen from up to forty miles out on the lake.

In 1759 the British captured Fort Niagara, one of the most valued prizes of the French and Indian War. Sailing traffic increased on the lake after the war; and by the early 1780s, the British had placed a beacon on top of the fort.

Recently retired, Fort Niagara Lighthouse has seen more than its share of history. Fur traders once gathered near here for the difficult overland portage to Lake Erie.

The purpose of the light was to prevent vessels sailing at night from running too far westward of Fort Niagara. A light is believed to have been kept in the tower only when a vessel was expected. Within a few years after the newly independent United States of America occupied Fort Niagara, in 1796, the fortress lighthouse was discontinued. The tower atop the fort is shown in drawings of the structure as late as 1803, but by 1806 it was gone.

Not until 1823 did another beacon, with a wooden tower, go into service atop the old French Castle. But two years later the Erie Canal was opened, and most of the river's east–west traffic was diverted away from the old Niagara Portage. The final blow to the commercial importance of the Niagara Portage came in 1829, when Canada opened its Welland Canal and commerce westward to the fast-growing city of Buffalo, on Lake Erie. Still, there was enough ship traffic on the Lake Ontario side of the Niagara River to warrant a light.

By the 1870s the Army began to find the light's location an inconvenience to daily life at the fort. It was abandoned in 1872, when a fifty-foot, octagonal stone tower was completed on the shore of Lake Ontario just south of the fort. In 1900 a lamp-oil shed was built and the tower was raised eleven feet to make the light visible twenty-five miles out into Lake Ontario. The additional tower space was used to house a watch room, which included a built-in desk for the keeper.

Edward Giddings, who was keeper of the light from 1823 to the early 1830s, participated in a major political incident of his day, the William Morgan Affair. Giddings and others were suspected of having murdered Morgan, a disgruntled Freemason who had threatened to reveal Masonic secret rites to the public. Shortly before he disappeared in 1826, Morgan was held by the Army at Fort Niagara, perhaps with the connivance of Giddings. News of this leaked to the press, precipitating a national scandal. Rumors of dark Masonic conspiracies could be heard on any street corner. Taking advantage of the furor, a small group of enterprising politicians founded the Anti-Masonic Party, an ephemeral player in the grand game of American national politics. As it turned out, the party was not so much anti-Masonic as it was anti-Andrew Jackson, who was then president of the United States as well as a Freemason. Ironically, William Wirt, the Anti-Masonic Party's presidential candidate in 1832, was himself a Freemason. He was soundly defeated by his fellow Freemason Jackson.

The attractions of Niagara Falls are ample and legendary, but visitors interested in human as well as natural history should set aside time for a trip to nearby Old Fort Niagara State Park.

The fort has served three nations and stands as a memorial to the grit and persistence of those who explored, fought for, and settled the new world. There are living history exhibits and numerous military reenactments during the summer.

The fort is open from mid-April through Labor Day, while the lighthouse is open weekends in June and then daily through Labor Day. Admission to the park and lighthouse exhibit is free. From Niagara, New York, follow the Robert Moses Parkway to the park entrance. Once inside the park, follow the signs to the lighthouse (recently deactivated by the Coast Guard). For more information call (716) 745–7611.

Like something out of a Jules Verne novel, Buffalo's famous bottle light marks the end of a stone pier. This W.C. Helbig photograph, provided courtesy of the National Archives, was taken in 1913.

CHAPTER TWO

LIGHTS OF
THE WARRIOR LAKE

Erie

Beauty, history, and function combine in this fine, old ship's wheel gracing the maritime museum of Fairport Lighthouse in Ohio. Such treats await visitors to lighthouse museums throughout the Great Lakes region.

Lights of the Warrior Lake

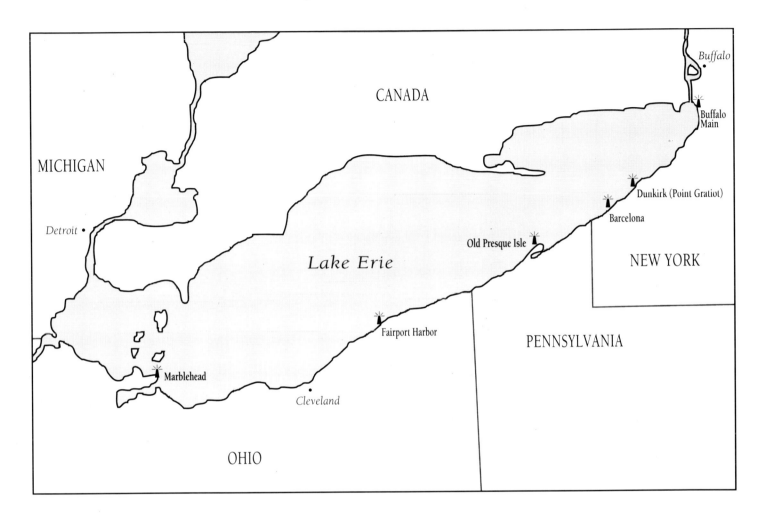

This harbor light station in Buffalo, pictured here as it appeared in 1914, is no longer standing. (Courtesy National Archives)

Generally speaking, lighthouses serve the mariners of all nations. But because they are built and maintained by governments, lighthouses are closely linked to political history. They have played important roles in the prosecution of war and in the making of nations.

As a builder of lighthouses, the United States is a world leader. We have more lighthouses along our inland shores (the shores of the Great Lakes) than most nations have on their entire ocean coastlines. This might not have been true, though, except for a rare freshwater naval battle fought more than 180 years ago.

BUCKSKINS AND TOMAHAWKS

On a September afternoon in 1813, backwoodsmen and farmers living in the remote northwestern corner of Ohio might have thought a storm had broken far out over the waters of Lake Erie. So it had, but the booming they heard in the distance was no natural thunder. Instead it was the roar of cannon, and the "storm" was a mighty sea battle being fought nearly 500 miles from the nearest salt water. Somewhere out there on the lake, a flotilla of heavily armed American warships and an equally powerful British fleet were slugging it out with steel and lead for control of Lake Erie and of the entire Great Lakes region.

One of only a very few naval engagements ever fought in fresh water, this extraordinary confrontation also proved to have been one of history's most decisive battles. The chain of events leading up to the Battle of Lake Erie began in a most unlikely way: with a bloody musket-and-tomahawk clash between buckskinned frontiersmen and Indians in war paint. In 1811 an army of pioneers, commanded by a flamboyant general named William Henry Harrison, ran head-on into a large Indian war party led by the legendary Tecumseh and his brother, "The Prophet." The battle erupted along an otherwise placid Indiana creek known to the Indians as Tippecanoe. When it was over, Tecumseh and his braves had been driven off, leaving behind many dead and a considerable number of British muskets.

Harrison's victory left an indelible mark on history. It opened up the midwestern states of Ohio, Indiana, and Illinois to a flood of white settlers, who now felt relatively safe from the Indians. It launched Harrison on a successful military and political career, which thirty years afterward would land him in the White House as the ninth president of the United States. In fact, Harrison campaigned for the presidency on the slogan "Tippecanoe and Tyler Too," a phrase that, to this day, still twists the tongues of grammar-school history students. But the battle's most immediate effect was to inflame American public opinion against the British, who were accused of supplying weapons to hostile western tribes. The anti-British sentiment grew to such a fever pitch that war was declared the following summer.

The decision to make war on the world's dominant naval power would quickly prove a disastrous one. The British swept American shipping from the seas, sealed off eastern ports, and even burned the White House and Capitol in Washington, D.C. Except for a brash twenty-eight-year-old naval lieutenant and his ragtag fleet on Lake Erie, the British might also have snatched away the vast lands to the south and west of the Great Lakes and given them to Canada.

When Lieutenant Oliver Hazard Perry arrived in Ohio during the autumn of 1812, he had no ships to command. His assignment of driving an already established British fleet from Lake Erie seemed hopeless. Perry's warships had to be built from scratch, using raw timber felled right on the shores of the lake.

As his small party of shipwrights and seamen labored around the clock, Perry kept a wary eye on the lakeward horizon. He was watching for sails signaling the British attack he was sure was coming to burn his unfinished ships, destroy his makeshift shipyard, and scatter his tiny force into the wilderness. But as construction of the American fleet continued, month after weary month, the British held back.

Commanding the British naval forces on the lake was Captain Robert Barclay, a veteran of the famed Battle of Trafalgar. Barclay felt secure at his base in Detroit, Michigan, and perhaps he took his young opponent too lightly. For whatever reason Barclay never attacked; and by the summer of 1813, Perry was able to complete and launch eight ships.

Early in September the American commander made his move. Having sailed his small fleet to the west end of Lake Erie, he blockaded the mouth of the Detroit River and cut off British supplies. Soon Barclay was forced to sail out and meet Perry on the open waters of the lake.

WE HAVE MET THE ENEMY

The battle, fought just to the west of Put-in-Bay and north of what is today the city of Sandusky, Ohio, commenced shortly before noon on September 10. The British cannon had longer range and began to blast away before the American ships could reply. But a favorable shift in the wind brought the two lines of embattled ships close together and allowed Perry's heavier short-range cannon to pound the enemy. Perry had filled the rigging of his largest vessels, the *Lawrence* and *Niagara*, with Kentucky long-riflemen, and their hawk-eyed sharpshooting picked off key British officers one by one. Although he would survive the battle, even Barclay fell, seriously wounded, on the deck of his flagship, the *Detroit*. By mid-afternoon the British were forced to strike their colors, and Perry, who would forever after be known as "Commodore Perry," was able to send his famous message back to the American shores: "We have met the enemy and they are ours; two ships, two brigs, one schooner, and one sloop."

Destruction of Barclay's fleet made it possible for General Harrison to march on Detroit and clear American territory of British outposts. In October he defeated the retreating British and their Indian allies, in a bitterly contested battle on Canadian soil. The entire British force was either killed or captured, and the charismatic Tecumseh was cut down while making a stubborn last stand with his braves.

An unexpected shift in the weather? Killer storms can strike suddenly on the Great Lakes, throwing up towering waves as dangerous as any on the open ocean.

Harrison's success on land, combined with Perry's victory out on Lake Erie, likely saved the Great Lakes states for the Americans. Without those states and the access to vital inland waterways they provided, the United States certainly would have been a much different, and poorer, country. By 1841, when Harrison became president, commerce generated by the Great Lakes region was already producing an economic boom. The Erie Canal linked the lakes to the Hudson and the Atlantic seaboard while a growing string of lighthouses led freighters and passenger steamers from Buffalo to Detroit and beyond.

As president, Harrison might have pushed for even more economic growth in the lakes region—perhaps ordering the construction of additional lighthouses—but he never got the chance. It rained on the day he took the oath of office. No longer the robust frontier soldier he had been during the War of 1812, Harrison was sixty-seven and in fragile health. While making what turned out to be the longest inauguration speech in history, he caught a severe cold. Ironically, little more than a month after taking office, the hero of Tippecanoe died from a fatal case of the sniffles.

BUFFALO MAIN LIGHT

Buffalo, New York – 1818 and 1833

With the opening of the Erie Canal in 1825, Buffalo began a hurly-burly boom that lasted well into the twentieth century and made this city near the eastern end of Lake Erie one of the busiest ports in the world. Political leaders had long recognized the commercial and strategic importance of the place. A light was planned for Buffalo's harbor as early as 1805, when Congress designated the village a port of entry. But action was delayed by tight-fisted New York legislators, who refused to share the cost of construction; and then by the British, who burned Buffalo during the War of 1812.

The Buffalo Main Lighthouse was finally completed and placed in operation in 1818, becoming one of the first two U.S. government lights on Lake Erie. A new, more powerful lighthouse was completed in 1833. Built at the end of a 1,400-foot-long pier, the buff-colored, octagonal limestone tower rose sixty-eight feet above the lake. Station improvements continued in 1856, with the addition of a fog bell. Simultaneously, a third-order Fresnel lens was installed in the tower. In 1866 both the Main Light and Pier Light underwent major renovations. By 1872 a major breakwater light station was in operation at the end of a recently completed 4,000-footlong breakwater. The breakwater light was fitted with a fourth-order fixed red light; and the fog bell (later to be replaced by a steam whistle) was moved from the main light to the new breakwater station.

A successful fund drive to restore the 1833 tower was begun in the early 1960s, and in 1985 the newly formed Buffalo Lighthouse Association began the project. In 1987 a replacement lens was relit in the restored tower, for the city's first International Friendship Festival.

Shaped something like the potbellied stove on the left, a delicate Fresnel lens (probably fourth-order) takes center stage in this turn-of-the-century Lighthouse Service Depot in Buffalo. Similar workshops throughout the Great Lakes region kept lighthouse lenses and equipment in top condition.
(Courtesy National Archives)

The Buffalo Main Lighthouse, bearing its date of construction, still stands today. Notice the bottle light in the background.

Overlooking the terminus of the Erie Canal, the Buffalo Lighthouse is located on the grounds of a Coast Guard station and is probably best viewed from the Naval and Service-man's Park, just across the river in downtown Buffalo. To reach the lighthouse, take I–190 to the Church Street exit, then turn right at the first stoplight onto Lower Terrace. Follow the signs to the Erie Basin Marina and Buffalo Main Lighthouse. For additional information call (716) 947–9126.

DUNKIRK (POINT GRATIOT) LIGHT
Point Gratiot, New York – 1829 and 1875

Dunkirk Lighthouse rises from a twenty-foot-high bluff at Point Gratiot, southwest of the Erie Canal terminus in Buffalo. Today it still throws its guiding beam across Lake Erie, just as it once did for nineteenth-century immigrant ships bound for the upper Great Lakes. Although its light helped keep vessels on course, it could not always prevent tragedy.

The first light at Dunkirk Harbor was commissioned in 1826, only a few years after one of the earliest recorded disasters on eastern Lake Erie. Launched in 1818 at Black Rock, New York, the paddlewheeler *Walk-In-The-Water* was the lake's first steamboat. But the power of steam could not altogether overcome the forces of nature, and in October 1818 this famous steamboat foundered on a sand bar in heavy weather.

The 132-foot long, thirty-two-foot-beam *Walk-In-The-Water* was en route from Buffalo and Detroit with a load of passengers and freight. Passage on the one-and-a-half-day cruise was $18 for a cabin and $7 for steerage. This particular trip turned

A glowing Fresnel lens at Dunkirk Lighthouse on Point Gratiot competes with the setting sun.

out not to be such a bargain; but, luckily, all the passengers were saved. Even the ship's huge steam engine was salvaged.

In 1841 the *Erie*, bound from Buffalo to Chicago, burned, with the loss of 141 lives, three miles east of Dunkirk. The tragedy was blamed on painters who had placed demijohns of turpentine and varnish on the deck immediately above the *Erie*'s boilers. The painters were riding the vessel as far as Erie, Pennsylvania, where they had a contract to paint the vessel S.S. *Madison*. In addition to her crew of thirty, the *Erie* carried 140 German and Swiss immigrants. The steamboat *De Witt Clinton*, which had just left Dunkirk, rescued twenty-seven survivors.

On October 14, 1893, the wooden steamboat *Dean Richmond*, named for a railway builder, foundered in heavy weather near Dunkirk. Built in Cleveland in 1864, the *Dean Richmond* made regular runs between Buffalo and Chicago. She left her last port of call—Toledo, Ohio—on October 13, 1893, with a cargo of bagged meal and flour, copper sheets, $50,000 worth of pig zinc, and $141,000 in gold and silver bullion. Gale-force winds battered her as she steamed eastward, and the unsecured copper sheets stowed on deck began to shift. The *Richmond* is believed to have tried to run in to Dunkirk just before she sank. Following the wreck area residents, including the keeper of the Dunkirk Lighthouse and his family, managed to salvage hundreds of bags of damp flour. It is said that, when the flour dried out, it made perfectly good bread.

The loss of the freighter *Idaho* off Dunkirk, during the late fall of 1897, brought a different sort of bounty to the area. The ship was carrying a large load of merchandise intended to be sold as Christmas presents, including a hefty store of chocolate, which washed ashore in large slabs. (No doubt children hereabouts had a very sweet Christmas that year.)

The first lighthouse at Gratiot Point, which became popularly known as Lighthouse Point, was completed in 1826 by Buffalo contractor Jesse Peck. It stood a short distance from the current sixty-one-foot-high tower, which replaced it in 1875.

Early attempts were made here to substitute natural gas for the whale oil typically used to fuel lighthouse lamps. These experiments were not successful, however. In 1857 the lantern was fitted with a third-order Fresnel lens, which produced a 15,000-candlepower flash every ninety seconds. The light could be seen from seventeen miles offshore.

Today the light station is leased to Chautauqua County Armed Forces Memorial Park Corporation, which operates it as a military museum. Point Gratiot is believed to be named for Charles Gratiot, the same U.S. Army engineer for whom Fort Gratiot, on Michigan's St. Clair River, is named.

The lighthouse complex, which included one of the famous bottle lights from Buffalo, is open daily from April through November and at other times upon request. The seven-room keeper's house now serves as one of the best lighthouse museums on the Great Lakes. Special events include War of 1812 reenactments, craft shows, and even lighthouse moonlight cruises. For further details call (716) 366–5050. The lighthouse is located in Dunkirk just off Route 5, which parallels the lakeshore just northwest of the New York State Thruway (I–90).

BARCELONA LIGHT

Barcelona, New York – 1829

Built in 1829 near a natural-gas–emitting spring, Barcelona Lighthouse became the first public building in the United States to be illuminated by gas. It is believed to have been the only lighthouse in the world ever to have been lighted with natural gas. Otherwise, the station had a short-lived and not overly distinctive career.

Its light extinguished before the Civil War, the stone tower of Barcelona Lighthouse still stands. The lantern was removed long ago, but the owners added a wooden framework at the top to suggest the tower's original function.

In 1828 Congress appropriated $5,000 to build a lighthouse on a bluff at what was then known as Portland Harbor, a community about twenty miles west of Dunkirk, New York. Completed the following year, it was fitted with oil lamps and a fourteen-inch reflector.

Three years later settlers in the area made an astonishing discovery: a pool of water that would, on occasion, catch fire. This "burning spring" produced natural gas, and inventive local folk soon found a way to put it to work. Placing a masonry cap over the gas well, they used wooden pipes to move the gas to the new Barcelona lighthouse. At the top of the tower, the gas was burned in specially designed lamps. The flame was so intense, it seemed to some sailors out on Lake Erie that the whole lighthouse was aflame. This rustic technology worked well enough for several years, until the flow from the gas well began to falter. After 1838 the well produced gas only sporadically, and the keeper was forced to use oil lamps instead.

The lighthouse was discontinued in 1859, when the government discovered a rather embarrassing error. The light had been intended to guide vessels into Barcelona's harbor. It was a good plan, but the fact was, Barcelona had no harbor. In time the Lighthouse Board sold the lighthouse for use as a private home.

Made of split native fieldstone, the forty-foot-high conical tower still stands. The tower and keeper's cottage are so attractive that they are often depicted on postcards. That they have survived the years speaks well for their early American workmanship. The cottage has stone walls twenty inches thick. According to the original specifications, the inside woodwork was "to be finished in a plain, decent style with good seasoned stuff."

Located just off I–90 on East Lake Road (Route 5) in Barcelona, the lighthouse is a private residence and not open to the public. Visitors are reminded not to trespass but to enjoy the lighthouse from the public right-of-way. Although the lantern was removed more than a century ago, a wooden-frame structure now simulates the lantern.

OLD PRESQUE ISLE LIGHT

Erie, Pennsylvania – 1819, 1867, and 1873

Originally, Pennsylvania had no shore frontage on Lake Erie, but the farsighted people of that friendly state recognized the importance of access to America's strategic inland seas. So, immediately after the Revolutionary War, they bought a forty-five-mile stretch of beaches and inlets with what turned out to be a very attractive and historic harbor. It was at Erie, Pennsylvania, that Perry and his shipwrights

built the modest flotilla of warships that defeated the powerful Great Lakes fleet of the British during the War of 1812.

Perhaps it was partly in memory of that victory, as well as in recognition of the growing importance of Erie as a port, that the government built the nation's second Great Lakes lighthouse in Pennsylvania. The light was placed on the Presque Isle Peninsula in 1819, to mark the entrance to Erie Bay. In French, the term *Presque Isle* means "not an island" and in this case apparently refers to the long, narrow peninsula. Shortly after the Civil War, this early lighthouse was replaced by a stately sandstone tower, which served lake sailors from 1867 until it was permanently discontinued in 1897. The old tower can still be seen in Erie's Dunn Park. Unfortunately, its original lantern room and dwelling were removed long ago.

The structure, known today as Presque Isle Light Station, was completed during the summer of 1873. It was fitted with a fourth-order Fresnel lens displaying a fixed white light. The sixty-eight-foot square tower placed the focal plane of the light seventy-three feet above the lake surface. The Fresnel lens has been replaced by an automated, airport–style beacon.

The active Presque Isle Lighthouse stands in Presque Isle State Park, at the end of a 7-mile-long finger of sand stretching into Lake Erie. From I–79, take Pennsylvania Alternate Route 5 West. At the fourth street light, turn right onto Route 832 (Peninsula Drive) and continue north 1½ miles to the park entrance. The lighthouse is located about 3 miles from the entrance. The Old Presque Isle Lighthouse, in Erie's Dunn Park on the mainland, recently had its lantern room replaced and is being restored.

FAIRPORT HARBOR LIGHT
Fairport, Ohio – 1825

Fairport Harbor, located midway between Cleveland and Ashtabula, was once the gateway to the old Western Reserve, owned by the state of Connecticut. Fairport's importance to Great Lakes shipping increased after 1803, when the new state of Ohio was formed from land relinquished by Connecticut and Virginia.

For countless immigrants bound for Michigan, Wisconsin, and Minnesota, the Fairport Harbor Light provided the first welcome glimpse of the American Midwest. Fairport long served as a refueling and supply port for passenger vessels and freighters bound westward from Buffalo, New York. The harbor's peak year before the Civil War was 1847, when 2,987 vessels transited the port, carrying $991,000 in

The sandstone tower of Fairport Lighthouse now seems out of place in its setting. The adjacent dwelling houses one of the Great Lakes' finest maritime museums.

cargo and an unknown number of passengers. The principal imports were farm wagons, furniture, cheese, flour, oil of peppermint, and, of course, people.

The light station at Fairport was completed in the fall of 1825, the same year the Erie Canal opened, connecting the Great Lakes with the Hudson River and the port of New York. Fairport's first lighthouse was built on the east side of the Grand River by Jonathan Goldsmith, a Connecticut native who had moved to Ohio in 1811. Goldsmith was awarded the contract for the lighthouse by A. W. Walworth, collector of customs for the district of Cuyahoga at Cleveland. A resident of Fairport, Walworth's father had been one of the earliest settlers of the Western Reserve. The senior Walworth had swapped houses with a Cleveland resident who believed that Fairport, not Cleveland, would be the area's major city.

The original brick tower was thirty feet high, with supporting walls three feet thick at the ground and twenty inches thick at the top. The tower was given an eleven-foot-diameter soapstone deck and capped with an octagonal-shaped iron lantern. The two-story keeper's house had spacious rooms, each with plastered walls, three windows, and a fireplace. There were also a sizable kitchen and cellar. The first keeper to live and work here was Samuel Butler.

By mid-century both the tower and keeper's cottage had badly deteriorated, and in 1869 Congress appropriated $30,000 to replace them. By August 1871 the station's third-order Fresnel lens had been installed in a new sandstone tower, where it shined for more than half a century.

On June 9, 1925, a combined-light-and-foghorn station was put in operation, and the federal government announced it would raze the old lighthouse. Local appeals to save the historic structure succeeded, and in 1941 the village of Fairport leased the lighthouse from the Coast Guard. Today the Fairport Harbor Historical Society maintains the lighthouse as a marine museum.

The museum in the old keeper's dwelling includes a wonderful collection of artifacts from the early days of the Lighthouse Service and a variety of other maritime exhibits. The museum is open 1:00–6:00 P.M. on Wednesdays, Saturdays, Sundays, and legal holidays from Memorial Day through Labor Day. For more information call (216) 354–4825. The museum is located at the northwest corner of Second and High streets in the village of Fairport Harbor. From US-20 at Painsville, follow either SR-283 or SR-535 to the village.

MARBLEHEAD LIGHT

Bay Point, Ohio – 1821

Built in 1821, Marblehead Lighthouse can boast the oldest active light tower on the Great Lakes. The Marblehead beacon has flashed out over a lot of history since it was placed in service, only a few years after Perry won his decisive victory over the British at the Battle of Lake Erie. This key naval battle was fought only a few miles to the north of Marblehead in September 1813, but that was not the last time war would touch the area.

The solid stone beach at the foot of Marblehead Lighthouse makes it easy to understand how this place got its name. Homesick Confederates in a nearby Civil War prison camp could see the light shining in this tower.

During the Civil War more than 10,000 Confederate soldiers languished in a 300-acre prison on Johnson's Island, within sight of the Marblehead Light. Most of the prisoners were officers captured in battles far to the south. No doubt these men frequently dreamed of their homes and farms in far-off Dixieland; but few, if any, ever escaped. At least one daring attempt, however, was made to free them.

On September 18, 1864, a small band of Confederate partisans commandeered the passenger steamer *Parsons* and headed for Johnson's Island. Apparently, they hoped to free some or all of the thousands of Confederate prisoners held there. Along the way the pirates encountered a second steamer, the *Island Queen*, and after a blazing gun battle, overwhelmed its crew. The *Island Queen* was eventually set adrift and the passengers and crew from both vessels put ashore on remote Middle Bass Island. Now totally in the hands of the commandos, the *Parsons* became what might very well be described as the only Confederate warship ever to serve on the Great Lakes. Unfortunately for the Southerners, the *Parsons* came up against the powerful Union gunboat *Michigan,* guarding the approach to Johnson's Island. Unable to challenge the *Michigan*'s heavy cannon, the Confederates turned the *Parsons* around and headed for the Detroit River. There they scuttled the steamer and escaped into Canada.

The Confederate prisoners on Johnson's Island may never have learned of the effort to free them. One thing they did learn, though, was the new sport of baseball. Residents of nearby Ohio communities taught them the rules. The Southerners proved very good at the game, regularly defeating Yankee teams who visited the island to play them. When they returned to the South following the war, the former prisoners took the sport with them. No doubt they also carried memories of their long imprisonment and of a light flashing every night on the shore as if to call them home.

The light they saw was, of course, the beacon of Marblehead Lighthouse, which over nearly one and three-quarters centuries has called countless thousands of sailors home from the lake. During all that time the old stone tower has changed very little. Late in the nineteenth century, its height was raised from fifty-five to sixty-five feet, but otherwise it looks much as it has since 1821. Fitted with a fourth-order Fresnel lens, it displays a flashing green light.

From Highway 2 at Port Clinton, take Route 163 to Marblehead. The light can be seen from a convenient parking area. The keeper's dwelling is used as a museum by the Ottawa County Historical Society. The grounds overlook the entrance to historic Sandusky Bay. For hours and other information, call the Ottawa County Visitors Bureau at (419) 734-4386.

CHAPTER THREE

LIGHTS OF
THE THUNDER LAKE

Huron

The **Cheboygan Crib Lighthouse** (at right) stands at the end of a short pier. It once stood offshore nearby, but the concrete-and-stone crib on which it stood settled into the lake, rendering it useless. The town of Cheboygan salvaged the old light and placed it on display in an attractive park at the end of Huron Street, east from US-23. From the pier you can also see the Poe Reef Lighthouse. **Round Island** (above) once kept its lonely vigil at the end of a meandering sand spit. Other reef lighthouses are difficult to view from land, and none are open to the public.

Lights of the Thunder Lake

DeTour Reef Lighthouse was built in 1931 over open water, as were all of Lake Huron's reef lighthouses. Cofferdams and massive piers often had to be constructed first. (Courtesy U.S. Coast Guard)

Why build lighthouses along the shores of the Great Lakes? For guidance. These lakes are no ordinary bodies of fresh water. They are enormous inland seas hundreds of miles in length. Sailors here need lighthouses to guide them, especially where low headlands offer few distinctive features. "It's like trying to navigate in a wheat field," said one frustrated sea captain after he brought his ocean-going freighter down the length of the St. Lawrence Seaway. But the Great Lakes lighthouses serve an even more important function—they save lives. In the wind torn waters of these lakes, safety is a vitally important consideration, and sailors keep a close eye on the weather. In a storm, lighthouses provide mariners with a comforting visual anchor.

THE STORMS OF NOVEMBER

November brings a marrow-deep chill to the bones of sailors on the Great Lakes. It's not just that the weather gets colder (it does, usually) but also that the lakes themselves take on a different character. They turn tempestuous and develop sharp, unpredictable tempers. Storms can blacken their faces in a matter of minutes and churn their waters into a confusion of towering waves capable of breaking a ship in half.

As the lakes change mood, so do the titanic commercial shipping enterprises they support. Captains and crews work overtime, hurrying to make one last trip; draw one last paycheck; or deliver one last cargo of iron, steel, oil, corn, or wheat before the witch of winter locks the lakes in a crush of unbreakable ice.

Tired sailors pushing themselves and their ships to the limit make a habit of looking back over their shoulders. They are watching for November—not the one on the calendar but the one that comes calling when you least expect it. Among Great Lakes sailors it is sometimes said that "Thanksgiving comes only if you survive November." They have endless tales of wreck and tragedy to prove the point: the November that took the *Fitzgerald* in 1975, the November that took the *Bradley* in 1958, and scores of other Novembers that sent stout ships and strong crews to the bottom. But when old lake sailors gather to tell stories of the calamities brought on by the year's eleventh month, there is one November they rarely leave out: November 1913.

Those who were superstitious about numbers said it would be an unlucky year; but up until the fall, 1913 had proved them wrong. The spring and summer had been kind to the Great Lakes, providing bathers, lovers, and sailors with a seemingly endless string of warm clear days and calm, starry nights. Business was booming, and the large and growing fleet of freighters operating on the lakes set records for shipping.

Then came October and, with it, high winds howling out of the west. A record cold snap sent temperatures plunging below zero, and a series of early snowstorms dusted the lakes shores with white. But for all its chill and bluster, October's unexpected outburst did little damage—a broken rudder here, a severed anchor chain there, and a couple of old wooden steamers run aground.

The year's fourth and final quarter had gotten off to an ominous start; but with lucrative contracts in their hands, captains were not willing to tie up their vessels for the season. They pushed themselves, their ships, and their crews harder than ever. They were determined to finish the work they had begun in the spring and continued so successfully during the summer, attempting to make 1913 the best year ever for shipping on the Great Lakes. But it was not to be.

At first November seemed likely to reverse the unsettling trend of the previous month. For a week gentle breezes rippled the lakes, and the temperatures were downright balmy. But experienced sailors knew these pleasant conditions would not hold for long, not at this time of year; and how right they were. Even as they hung their uniform jackets to enjoy the unseasonable temperatures in shirt-sleeves while their freighters cut through glassy-smooth water, three deadly weather systems were headed their way. One rushed in with freezing winds from the Bering Sea; another poured over the Rockies, carrying an immense load of water from as far off as the South Pacific; and a third came spinning up, cyclone–style, from the Caribbean.

Subzero winter temperatures can turn lake water as hard as concrete, which made it possible for this car to visit Poe Reef Lighthouse in 1937. (Courtesy U.S. Coast Guard)

The three slammed into one another over the Great Lakes on or about November 7, 1913, creating what was in effect an inland hurricane.

This extraordinary storm struck with little or no warning. Dozens of freighters were caught in mid-lake, far from safe anchorage; or worse, near ship-killing rocks, shoals, and shallows. High waves battered hulls, and freezing spray caked decks and wheelhouses in a thick layer of ice. Swirling snow squalls blinded captains, pilots, and navigators, while high winds drove their vessels ever closer to disaster. The storm raged on without pause for five long days. By the time the clouds broke and the winds died down, on November 12, more than forty ships had been wrecked, their hulls shattered by the waves or ripped open on shoals. Down with them went 235 sailors and passengers. Only a few of the bodies were ever recovered.

GOOD-BY NELLIE

On Lake Erie the 187-ton *Lightship No. 82* was blown off its mooring and bowled over by the waves. All six crewmen were lost. Before he drowned, Captain Hugh Williams apparently scratched a hurried farewell to his wife on a piece of wood and set it adrift. A waterlogged board later found washed up on a beach in New York held this message: "Good-by Nellie, ship breaking up fast. Williams."

Up on Lake Superior the tramp freighter *Leafield* was driven onto rocks and torn to pieces. All eighteen members of the crew were lost. Also lost on Superior was the 525-foot ore freighter *Henry B. Smith*. In a tragic lapse of judgment and prudent seamanship, Captain Jimmy Owen took the *Smith* out of the relative safety of Marquette Harbor and steamed directly into the teeth of the storm. Only a few scattered pieces of wreckage, and none of the ship's twenty-three crewmen, were ever found.

It was on Lake Huron, however, that the storm vented its full fury. When the storm first assaulted Huron on November 7, its shipping lanes were filled with vessels crossing northwestward toward Michigan and Superior or southeastward toward Erie. As darkness set in, lighthouse beacons called to these ships from many points along the Michigan shore. There were safe harbors in this storm, and the lights marked the way. But most ships could not reach them or make any headway at all against the fierce westerly winds. Many captains pointed their bows toward the northeast and made a run for the Canadian side, where they hoped to find some protection. Many never made it.

Huron's mountainous waves chewed up dozens of ships, and the lake's deep waters swallowed them whole. At least eight large freighters—the *McGean*, *Carruthers*, *Hydrus*, *Wexford*, *Scott*, *Regina*, *Price*, and *Argus*—all disappeared from the lake without a trace. Vanishing with them were 178 passengers and crewmen.

FORT GRATIOT LIGHT

Port Huron, Michigan – 1825 and 1829

Established in 1825, the Fort Gratiot Light Station is Michigan's oldest—older, in fact, than the state itself, which was admitted to the Union in 1837. Today, nearly one and three-quarters centuries after its light first guided sailors, the station still keeps watch over the Lake Huron entrance to the St. Clair River. A short distance upstream is the lightship *Huron*, in the city of Port Huron's Pine Grove Park. The last U.S. lightship to serve on the Great Lakes, it is a National Historic Landmark.

The first keeper of the Fort Gratiot Lighthouse was George McDougal, a Detroit lawyer who won his appointment through political influence. His was not a plum job, however, as McDougal depleted his personal savings keeping the station

habitable. The tower was not built to government specifications, the materials used were shoddy, and McDougal considered it unsafe. He was correct. The tower fell down, and a more robust structure replaced it in 1829.

Today the tower stands more than eighty feet tall. Automated in 1933, its light has a focal plane eighty-six feet above lake level. The thick-walled conical stone tower, overlaid with red brick, has been painted white. The keeper's cottage and fog whistle house are red brick. Atop the tower a red dome covers the lantern room.

The Fort Gratiot Lighthouse is older than the state of Michigan itself. That's Canada in the background.

From I–94 take Pine Grove Street (M-25) north, then turn right onto Garfield Street and follow it to Gratiot Avenue. The lighthouse, open only a few times a year, is located on a Coast Guard facility. Parking is available in the area. For information on tours call (313) 982–0891 or ask at the nearby Huron Lightship Museum.

LIGHTSHIP HURON

Port Huron, Michigan – 1921

Unlike the nearby Fort Gratiot Lighthouse, which has stood its ground for many years, the lightship *Huron* has had a highly mobile history. The keel for the *Huron* was laid by The Charles Seabury Company of Morris Heights, New York, in 1921, at the end of World War I. Commissioned as Lightship No. 103 by the U.S. Lighthouse Service, it began its career as a relief lightship for Lake Michigan's Twelfth Lighthouse District. When other light-

ships had to be brought in for repairs, the *Huron* took over their station. After fourteen years of relief duty, Lightship No. 103 was assigned first to Gray's Reef, Michigan, on Lake Michigan's east coast and then to Manitou Shoals on northern Lake Michigan. In 1935 the ninety-seven-foot vessel was placed on station at Corsica Shoals in Lake Huron, where it was a beacon for shipping bound to and from the St. Clair River.

At night and in storms, the light from the *Huron*'s fifty-two-foot, six-inch-high lantern mast guided vessels into and out of the narrow, dredged channel, enabling large vessels to transit the river and lower Lake Huron. A 5,000-pound mushroom anchor kept the 310-ton, twenty-four-foot-beam lightship at her position, six miles north of the Blue Water Bridge over the St. Clair River in Port Huron and three miles east of the Michigan mainland.

In 1949 the lightship was refitted in Toledo, Ohio. The steam engine was replaced by diesels and radar, and a radio beacon and fog signal were added. Despite a 1945 Coast Guard directive that all lightship hulls be red, the *Huron* kept its black color. HURON was painted on its side in large block letters.

After being decommissioned in 1970, the *Huron* was acquired by the city of Port Huron. The lightship now serves as a museum, operated by the nearby Museum of Arts and History with support from the Lake Huron Lore Marine Society. Nearby Fort Gratiot Light can be viewed from Lighthouse Park.

Enshrined since 1972 in Pine Grove Park in Port Huron, the lightship Huron *is open 1:00–4:30 P.M. from Wednesday through Sunday in July and August and on weekends in May, June, and September. For information call (313) 982–0891. From I–94 drive south on Pine Grove Street (M-25), turn left on Prospect Street, and follow it one block to the lightship parking area. The* Huron *is located beside the water at the north end of Pine Grove Park.*

POINTE AUX BARQUES LIGHT
Port Austin, Michigan – 1848 and 1857

The French called the place *Pointe Aux Barques,* or "Point of Little Boats," perhaps because of the many canoes brought here by fur traders. This strategic headland marks a key turning point from Lake Huron into Saginaw Bay. Recognizing its importance to shipping, the federal government chose Pointe Aux Barques as the site for one of tallest and most powerful lighthouses on the Great Lakes.

As beautiful as it is useful, the Point Aux Barques Lighthouse still guides mariners. Its bright white tower makes an excellent daymark. As its French name suggests, this point has long been vital to shipping.

Completed in 1848 at a cost of $5,000, the original stone structure proved inadequate and had to be rebuilt less than ten years later. In 1857 it was replaced with an impressive eighty-nine-foot brick tower, fitted with a state-of-the-art, third-order Fresnel lens imported from France. Today this beautiful old lens can be seen at the Grice Museum in Port Austin. Its work is now being done by a 1 million-candlepower automated beacon. The flashing white light can be seen from about eighteen miles out in Lake Huron.

For many years Pointe Aux Barques also had an active lifesaving station. During the great November storm of 1913, the steamer *Howard M. Hanna* foundered near here. The station crew managed to save thirty-three of the *Hanna*'s passengers and crew. The station is now part of a very interesting museum complex in Huron City depicting life as it was lived here during the nineteenth century.

The Pointe Aux Barques Lighthouse is located in a county park off Lighthouse Road, about 10 miles east of Port Austin and 6 miles north of Port Hope. Take M-25 to Lighthouse Road. The keeper's dwelling houses a museum and gift shop, open on weekends from noon until 4:00 P.M. Memorial Day through Labor Day. The tower is not open to public, but park visitors enjoy excellent views of the light. The park offers a campground and picnic area.

The Huron City Museum, which houses many nineteenth-century displays and exhibits, is less than a mile to the northwest of the lighthouse and can be reached from M-25 via Huron City Road. Museum hours are 10:00 A.M. to 5:00 P.M. daily (except Tuesday) from July 1 through Labor Day. For museum information call (517) 428–4123.

TAWAS POINT LIGHT
Tawas City, Michigan – 1853 and 1876

The thumb of Michigan's mitten is created by a long, southwestern extension of Lake Huron called Saginaw Bay. By the middle of the nineteenth century, the bay had become commercially strategic, and lighthouse officials saw the need to mark its entrance. In 1848 they placed a lighthouse at Pointe Aux Barques on the south side of the entrance, and five years later another was built at Ottawa Point (now known as Tawas Point) on the north side. The Tawas Point Lighthouse was completed and in operation by 1853, but its beacon served mariners for little more than twenty years.

Lake Huron constantly reshapes certain sections of its shoreline. By the 1870s sandy Tawas Point had grown so much that the lighthouse stood more than a mile from the waters of the lake. To correct this problem the Lighthouse Board asked Congress for a $30,000 appropriation to build a new lighthouse. The sixty-seven-foot tower was completed and in operation by 1875. The conical tower is painted white and is topped by a black iron lantern room. The flashing white beacon is produced by a rotating fourth-order Fresnel lens.

To protect keepers from the weather, the brick dwelling was connected to the tower by a narrow brick passageway. Today the lighthouse serves as residence for a high-ranking Coast Guard officer.

The lighthouse is located in Tawas Point State Park. To reach the lighthouse drive about 1 1/2 miles west of Tawas City on US-23, then turn right onto Tawas Beach Road. Continue into the park and drive to the beach parking area at the end of the road. Follow the walking path to the lighthouse, which can be seen from the parking area. The tower is open to the public in June, and the Coast Guard offers tours during most summer months. For information on tours call (517) 362–4429. Camping facilities and picnic tables are available in the park.

A fourth-order Fresnel lens lights up the lantern room atop Tawas Point Lighthouse.

STURGEON POINT LIGHT
Alcona, Michigan – 1869

Beaming from the top of a sixty-eight-foot light tower, Sturgeon Point Lighthouse has saved many lives since it was placed in service in 1870. Today the light continues to guide mariners and warn them away from a nearby ship-killing reef. Although the light station remains active, nowadays it serves as a museum. Occasionally, visitors can climb the eighty-five steps of the tower's cast-iron stairway.

Bright colors and stark contrasts give this spring view of Sturgeon Point Lighthouse a Mediterranean look.

Standing beside the 3.5-order lens inside the lantern room and gazing out across the lake, one is reminded of the life-or-death dramas that have taken place in this dangerous stretch of water.

On August 27, 1880, the wooden steamer *Marine City* took on a cargo of shingles at Alcona. Along with the shingles came three Detroit-bound stowaways, who apparently had concealed themselves in the cargo hold. Their passage would not be free, however. In fact, they would pay dearly for it. For two hours the *Marine City* made good time in a freshening breeze that kicked up white-capped waves on the lake. Then calamity struck. Smoke and flames were seen coming from the hurricane deck near its juncture with the ship's funnel. Passengers rushed to either side of the ship's weather deck as flames began to engulf the tinderbox superstructure.

A pair of tugboats were the first rescue vessels at the scene. When her captain saw the smoke, the tugboat *Vulcan* steamed at top speed toward the *Marine City*. Just exiting the Black River, the tugboat *Grayling* cut loose the barge she was towing and set out in the wake of the *Vulcan*. The Sturgeon Point Lifesaving crew as well as John Pasque, the lighthouse keeper, joined in the rescue effort. Of 121 passengers and crew aboard the *Marine City*, all but twenty were rescued. Among those thought to have died in the flames were the three stowaways.

There have been many disasters and near-disasters in the vicinity of Sturgeon Point. In October 1887 the 233-ton schooner *Venus*, loaded with grindstones, foundered off Black River, with the loss of seven lives. In 1903 the crew of the three-masted schooner *Ispeming* were forced to abandon ship. Fortunately, all were rescued by a tug.

A tragedy unseen except by those who perished occurred in September 1924, when the vessel *Clifton*, loaded with stone, disappeared during a fierce gale that swept Lake Huron. The last recorded sighting of *Clifton* was at 7:00 A.M. on the same day the vessel cleared Old Mackinac Point. Following the storm wreckage was found off Black River, forty-five miles southeast of Alpena. Among the debris were an empty raft and a pilothouse clock, which had stopped at 4:00 P.M.

Automated in 1936, the Sturgeon Point Light Station was purchased and renovated by the Alcona County Historical Society. The keeper's quarters house museum exhibits. On display on the grounds outside is the big rudder salvaged from the *Marine City*.

The museum in the keeper's house is open daily from Memorial Day to Labor Day. During the fall color season, the museum is open weekends. For exact hours and other information call (517) 724–6297. To reach the lighthouse take US-23 north from Harrisville, then turn right on Point Road. The parking lot for the lighthouse is located less than a mile down the road. This is one of the most inviting lighthouses on the Great Lakes for photography.

LIGHTHOUSES OF PRESQUE ISLE

Presque Isle, Michigan – 1840 and 1871

Built in 1870 on a peninsula jutting into Lake Huron and still guiding vessels to this day, the New Presque Isle Light beams from one of the highest towers on the Great Lakes. Now automated, the light was authorized in the 1860s by President Abraham Lincoln. Its beacon is visible for twenty-five miles and is still used as a bearing by commercial vessels bound for Lakes Michigan and Superior.

The New Presque Isle Lighthouse soars 113 feet above its placid surroundings. The attached dwelling suggests a farmhouse.

The 113-foot light tower and the attached rectangular brick keeper's house are the centerpiece for a 100-acre public park maintained by Presque Isle Township. The park also includes Old Presque Isle Lighthouse, which was completed in 1840 and discontinued in 1871, when the new tower took over its duties. There are also range lights, which were used to mark the harbor channel. These venerable structures occupy a cedar- and pine-covered peninsula that helps form Presque Isle Harbor on one side and North Bay on the other side.

The need for a lighthouse on the peninsula was recognized during the early 1830s, when an increasing number of commercial vessels began using Presque Isle Harbor for shelter as well as for a source of cordwood to fire their boilers. After Congress appropriated $5,000 to build a light station, the contract for the thirty-foot-high, stone-and-brick light tower and a keeper's cottage was awarded to Jeremiah Moors of Detroit, who completed the work in September 1840. The first keeper was Henry L. Woolsey. Patrick Garrity took over some twenty-one years afterward, at the beginning of the Civil War.

In March 1869.Congress appropriated $7,500 to construct range lights on shore to mark the channel for vessels bound in and out of the harbor. The front range light was housed in a fifteen-foot-high, octagonal wood-frame structure. The rear light was located about 800 feet away and thirty-six feet above lake level. Both range lights have been discontinued. The rear range lighthouse is now a private residence.

New Presque Isle Light and its cottage were completed in 1871; Garrity and his wife, Mary, happily moved from the old keeper's dwelling to the more spacious new one. The gable-roofed house was connected to the tower by an enclosed walk-

The Old Presque Isle Lighthouse is said by some to be haunted.

way. During their tenure at the two stations, the Garritys reared numerous children. Daughter Anna is said to have maintained night-long vigils looking out over the lake from a rocking chair at the rear range light.

The tower base is nineteen feet, three inches tall and is capped with an iron

watchroom and a ten-sided cast-iron lantern, which still contains its original third-order Fresnel lens crafted by Henri Lepaute of Paris. In the late 1980s the tower was restored to its original condition. Extensive work has also been done to the keeper's cottage. Both are open seasonally to the public.

In 1885 Thomas Garrity took over from his father and was keeper of New Presque Isle Light until 1935, a remarkable fifty-year tenure. Coastguardsmen tended the station from 1939 until the early 1970s, when the light was automated and the keeper's house boarded up.

There is a persistent story about a lighthouse ghost, said to be that of a keeper's wife (not Mrs. Garrity) driven insane by the isolation. Supposedly, she was locked up permanently by her husband. Some say that, on windy nights, you can hear the screams of a woman coming from inside one of the lighthouses (it's not clear which).

Spiral steps climb toward the lantern room at Old Presque Isle Lighthouse.

From Presque Isle follow Grand Lake Road past the intersection of Highway 638, or from US-23 take Highway 638 to Grand Lake Road and turn left. A little more than half a mile to the north are the Old Presque Isle Lighthouse and Museum. A pair of range light towers stands nearby. From the museum continue north about one mile on Grand Lake Road to the New Presque Isle Lighthouse, which is surrounded by a scenic, 100-acre park. There is also a fine museum and gift shop here. The four lighthouses (old and new, front and rear range) offer the visitor an especially valuable lesson in lighthouse history and lore.

FORTY MILE POINT LIGHT

Rogers City, Michigan – 1897

Until the late 1890s the fifty-mile stretch of shoreline between Cheboygan and Presque Isle Lighthouse was dark and threatening to mariners. Here was a gap in an otherwise almost unbroken chain of navigational lights guiding ships through the Great Lakes. In 1894 Congress decided to fill the gap and appropriated $25,000 for a light station at Forty Mile Point.

Completed in 1896 and placed in operation the following year, the square brick tower stands fifty-three feet tall. At the top an octagonal, black-trimmed cast-iron lantern contains a fourth-order Fresnel lens displaying a flashing white light. Painted white, the tower stands in sharp contrast to the attached natural-brick keeper's dwelling.

The architecture of the two-story dwelling is quite interesting and features a pair of dormers, one on either side of the tower. The station also has a well-preserved brick oil house and fog-signal building.

Down on the beach below the lighthouse is the rotting hulk of a wooden ship wrecked here in the distant past. Visitors often walk the beach looking for pudding-stones (the remnants of a volcanic eruption many millions of years ago).

The well-maintained tower, dwelling, and other structures are not open to the public at this time, but the grounds and buildings are quite beautiful and well worth a visit. About 6 miles north of Rogers City on US-23, you will encounter a sign directing you to Presque Isle County Lighthouse Park. Turn right onto an otherwise unmarked road and follow it to the lighthouse (do not take Forty Mile Point Road).

As ships approach the Straits of Mackinac from the Lake Huron side, they enter one of the most dangerous stretches of water in the Great Lakes or perhaps anywhere. Here the broad waters of Lake Huron narrow down to just a few miles in width, and ships squeezing through this area must run an obstacle course of treacherous shallows and ship-killing reefs.

*Among the most deadly of these is **Spectacle Reef** (above, courtesy U.S. Coast Guard), a pair of clawlike shoals lurking a few feet below sea level. The loss of two large schooners here in 1867 spurred demands from sailors and shipping interests that something be done to mark these vicious shoals. Soon afterward Congress appropriated $100,000 to build a lighthouse directly over the shoals. A princely sum for the time, the appropriation would prove inadequate.*

*Two lighthouse tenders and more than 200 men worked for nearly four years to complete the project. When it was finally finished in 1874, it had cost taxpayers some $406,000. More than 120 years later, its (now solar-powered) light still serves lake sailors. The tower contains the original second-order Fresnel lens. The government eventually built lighthouses on several other dangerous shoals near the straits, among them **Round Island**, **Poe Reef**, **Fourteen Foot Shoal**, and **DeTour Point**. All lighthouses contain their original Fresnel lenses, and all have been automated.*

OLD MACKINAC POINT LIGHT
Mackinaw City, Michigan – 1892

When the bridge over the Straits of Mackinac opened in 1957, Old Mackinac Point Light was no longer needed. Vessels that once took bearings from the forty-foot-tall turn-of-the-century light began ranging on the bridge's lights instead. In 1960 the lighthouse was converted into a maritime museum, as part of a twenty-seven-acre historical park operated by the Mackinac Island State Park Commission.

The light at Mackinaw City, which guided vessels through the straits connecting Lake Michigan and Lake Huron, evolved from a fog-signal station that first went into operation in November 1890. During one especially foggy stretch in its second year of operation, the fog signal was run for 327 hours, the boilers consuming fifty-two cords of wood.

In the late nineteenth century, Great Lakes shipping rapidly increased in volume. Vessels got bigger and technology more sophisticated. The existing Straits of Mackinac sentinels at McGulpin's Point and St. Helena Island were considered inadequate, under certain circumstances, for vessels approaching from the west. The need for a light at Old Mackinac Point became apparent almost as soon as the fog signal was completed.

A colorful roof gives the Old Mackinac Point Lighthouse a festive appearance. This light once marked the heavily trafficked Straits of Mackinac, which connects lakes Michigan and Huron. Today the building houses a maritime museum.

The lights of Mackinac Bridge, shown here reaching into the distance, now mark the straits for shipping. Once the bridge opened in 1957, the nearby lighthouse was no longer needed.

On March 3, 1891, Congress appropriated $20,000 to build a lighthouse. The buff-colored brick tower and attached keeper's dwelling were completed on October 27, 1892. The fourth-order lens light atop the tower had gone into service on the night of October 25, 1892.

At about the same time that the lighthouse was built, federal officials decided to move the fog signal. The new site for the signal intruded into a park recently established by Mackinaw City. Unable to persuade the villagers to give up their park, federal authorities condemned the land. The village fought the condemnation, creating a legal snarl not resolved until 1905, when the federal government agreed to pay Mackinaw City $400 for the land. In 1906 the fog-signal building was finally moved to its new site and was later replaced by a brick building. By the mid-twentieth century, a 132-foot-high radio beacon tower was erected beside the old brick fog-signal building.

From exit 336 off I–75, follow Nicolet Avenue through Mackinaw City, then turn right on Huron Avenue. About 2 blocks down is the parking area for the Old Mackinac Point Lighthouse. The area around the lighthouse is a lovely park with plenty of picnic tables and a wonderful view of the Mackinac Bridge. The nearby Riviera on the Beach Motel provides a romantic spot for an overnight stay and a leisurely enjoyment of the lighthouse and bridge.

CHAPTER FOUR

LIGHTS OF
THE ALL-AMERICAN LAKE

Michigan

Many Great Lakes lighthouses are built offshore and are connected to the land by long piers or catwalks. Several fine examples of this type of lighthouse can be seen along the eastern shores of Lake Michigan. Most are located within a day's drive of one another just a few miles off U.S. 31 in western Michigan State. Among the most striking of Michigan's pier lighthouses are those marking the entrance to the Grand River and one of the state's best deepwater harbors. Known as the **Grand Haven South Pier Inner Light** and the **Grand Haven South Pierhead Light**, they stand several hundred feet apart on a long stone pier. The inner light was built in 1895 and consists of a fifty-one-foot steel cylinder topped by a small lantern. The squat pierhead light was originally the fog-signal building and was moved to its current location when the pier was extended in 1905. A tiny lantern nestles on the roof. The wooden structure has been sheathed in iron to protect it from Lake Huron's destructive, storm-driven waves.

Lights of the All-American Lake

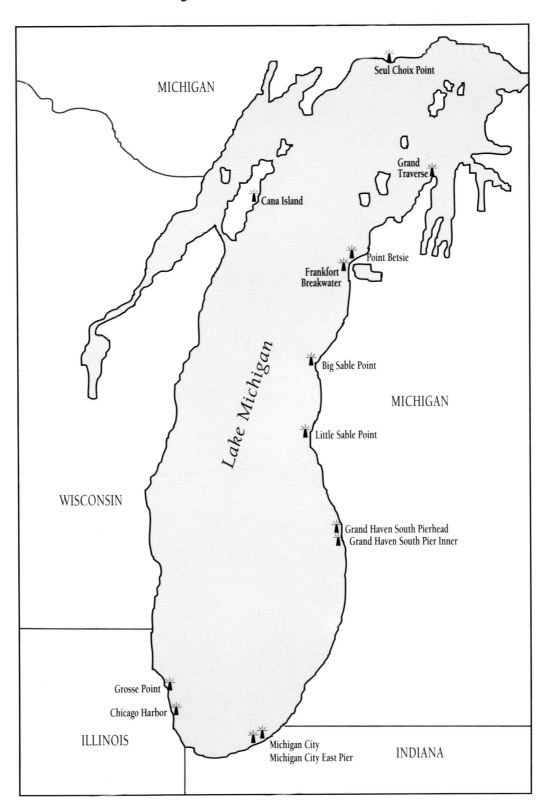

MICHIGAN

Seul Choix Point

Grand
Traverse

Cana Island

Point Betsie

Frankfort
Breakwater

Big Sable Point

MICHIGAN

Little Sable Point

WISCONSIN

Grand Haven South Pierhead
Grand Haven South Pier Inner

Lake Michigan

Grosse Point

Chicago Harbor

ILLINOIS

Michigan City
Michigan City East Pier

INDIANA

Mariners in upper Lake Michigan are happy to see Seul Choix Lighthouse, looming here in the background. Feathered navigators prefer the lighthouse on the right.

The Lighthouse Service once maintained a small fleet of tenders to carry food, fuel, equipment, spare parts, and personnel to isolated light stations. Lighthouse tenders were usually named after flowers, trees, and shrubs. During the early decades of this century, the tender *Hyacinth*, operating out of Milwaukee and Chicago, served many of the lake lighthouses, especially those on Lake Michigan. Lighthouse keepers were always happy to see the *Hyacinth* steaming toward them with its cargo of fresh food and much-needed supplies. No doubt the lonely keepers were also glad to have visitors and enjoyed sharing news, a scrap or two of gossip, and a hot mug of coffee with the captain and crew of the *Hyacinth*.

A SEA DOG RETURNS TO THE WATER

For many years the most welcome and best-loved member of the *Hyacinth* crew was a sailor known to one and all only as "Sport." While some lake sailors may complain, rightly or wrongly, of living a dog's life, Sport never voiced such a grievance. He was, in fact, a dog who lived a sailor's life.

For more than a dozen years, Sport, a spotted mongrel, sailed with the *Hyacinth*, making friends everywhere he went. When he died of old age, he was buried in Lake Michigan with full seaman's honors. The following elegy appeared in the September 1926 *Lighthouse Bulletin* (published by the U.S. Lighthouse Service, Department of Commerce).

> *To the Superintendent of Lighthouses, Milwaukee, Wisconsin*
>
> *Sport was just a dog, but he was always a good dog and a good ship-mate, a friend to everybody and everybody's friend. I do not think he had an enemy and I am certain that he had more friends, or perhaps I should say acquaintances, around the shores of Lake Michigan than any man on this ship today.*
>
> *Sport came on board this vessel back in 1914 when engineer Albert Collins pulled him out of the Milwaukee River during a thunderstorm. He was in a pitiful condition and practically skin and bones. He was rescued and fed, and apparently, from that moment on, never had a notion to leave the ship.*
>
> *Many things have happened to Sport and he has figured in many happenings aboard the ship in the 12 years he spent on board, which is longer than any officer or member of the crew has been here. It will not do to go into all the details of his life for they are many.*

It is enough to say that when he was in his prime there was no place on the ship that he did not visit and nothing going on that he did not have a hand or paw in. He swam and played baseball with the boys. No boat could go ashore without Sport, and on many occasions he has carried a heaving line to shore in the breakers when landing on the beach at some light station with our crew.

He was lost in Chicago on one occasion and could not be found. We were a sad lot when we left Chicago without him and a happy lot when . . . the captain of the passenger steamer Indiana *called me on the telephone to tell me he had Sport on board and to come over and get him. It was learned afterwards that someone had tied him up in a barn in Chicago, and it so happened that a man who had been a fireman on board (the* Hyacinth) *was driving an ice wagon and found Sport and brought him back to our Chicago pier keeper who in turn gave him to Captain Redner on the* Indiana *to deliver to us in Milwaukee. All of which goes to show that he had friends everywhere.*

Sport died of old age on July 19, 1926. He was sewed in canvas and buried at sea the afternoon of the following day two miles off Ludington, Michigan. All hands were mustered on the spar deck where, with a few words for Sport to the effect that he had been taken from the waters and was now being returned to them, he was slid off the gangplank by a bunch of solemnlooking boys. He was given a salute and thus ended Sport, the best dog I have ever known."

Sport was not the only one pulled out of a cold river by a *Hyacinth* seaman. At about the time the old sea dog took his last journey, his friends on the *Hyacinth* were making a whole series of daring rescues. In 1925 oiler Everett Wynoble jumped overboard into the freezing waters of the Chicago River to save a drowning woman. The following year in Green Bay, Wisconsin, fireman Louis Ettenhoffer performed the same service for a six-year-old boy who had fallen out of a small boat. It was early evening and Ettenhoffer was going ashore to enjoy what for him was a rare treat—a home-cooked meal at his sister's house in Green Bay. No sooner had his feet hit the dock than he noticed the struggling child. Ettenhoffer was himself a very poor swimmer, but he jumped into the river immediately and grabbed the boy just in time to keep him from sinking. Somehow he reached a piling and held on to it with one hand and the boy with the other until both could be rescued by other members of the *Hyacinth* crew.

In his report on the incident, the *Hyacinth*'s master, Captain H. W. Maynard, noted that "the boy had swallowed some water but was not harmed." As for Ettenhoffer, said the captain, "He had done about all the swimming he was capable of doing and had consumed a great plenty of the Fox River's water. He, however, changed his clothes and kept his dinner engagement."

Later in 1926, while tied up at a dock to service a lighthouse at Sturgeon Bay, Wisconsin, the *Hyacinth* almost became the first lighthouse tender to be hit by a

The elegant tower of Grosse Point Lighthouse rises far above spreading tree limbs on a quiet residential street in suburban Evanston, Illinois. The campus of Northwestern University is nearby.

car. Crewmen heard the roar of an engine and looked up in astonishment from their chores to see an automobile racing along the pier and bearing down on their ship. Luckily, the speeding car missed the *Hyacinth*; but, unfortunately for the driver, it ran right off the end of the dock into Sturgeon Bay. Although the car sank immediately, crewmen could see its lights still burning under the water. Working quickly, they managed to snare the vehicle with a grappling hook and use the tender's hoist to pull the car out of the bay. Unhappily, their efforts were not in time to save the hapless driver. No one ever knew why he drove his car off the dock.

Working on a lighthouse tender could be quite dangerous. Over the years many seamen lost their lives in the line of duty. Occasionally, sailors were drowned when swells overturned the small boats they used for landing passengers and supplies at remote lighthouses. Others were killed while trying to rescue the crews of wrecked ships. Some died in falls or when swept overboard by high waves. A few lost their lives while doing routine work on the tenders themselves. In 1914 seaman John Larson suffered a particularly ghastly death when a gasoline blowtorch blew up. When the fiery explosion occurred, Larson was holding the torch between his legs and using it to burn paint off the bulwarks of the tender *Marigold*.

DISASTER ON LAKE MICHIGAN

While not so stormy as Lake Superior and not so narrow and difficult to navigate as Lake Erie, Lake Michigan has seen far more than its share of catastrophes. In fact, its list of disasters includes several of the most deadly accidents in the history of the Great Lakes. The worst among these tragedies came on the morning of July 24, 1915, less than two years after the massive storm of November 1913 and only three years after the sinking of the *Titanic*. Most Great Lakes sinkings, especially those with a high cost in human lives, are caused by gales, collisions, or fire. But not this one. Ironically, the ship involved was still at its dock.

The sun streamed down onto the Clark Street Pier in Chicago as the steamer *Eastland* took on a heavy load of 2,500 passengers, most of them Western Electric employees and their families going on a holiday. The mood was festive, and the *Eastland*'s steam calliope kept everyone tapping their feet, clapping their hands, and singing.

The merriment continued as the gangplank came up and a tug started to pull the *Eastland* away from the dock. She moved only a few feet, however, and then began to tilt over on her port side. Someone noticed that the lines near the stern had not been released, and it was too late now to cast them off. The tug had pulled them taut, and the harder it pulled, the farther the *Eastland* tilted.

Sensing danger, the passengers panicked and crowded over onto the port side, adding their enormous combined weight to the force of the tug. Soon the ship was settling into the harbor, dumping a screaming mass of humanity into the water as she went. Little more than twenty feet deep, the harbor slip was too shallow to cover the *Eastland*'s hull, but that fact did scarcely anything to lessen the plight of the struggling passengers. Thrown willy-nilly into the harbor one atop the other, most victims had little chance to save themselves. Even good swimmers were carried down in the flailing crush. When all the bodies were counted, the death toll came to an incredible 835. almost exactly a third of those on board.

A lifetime before the *Eastland* tragedy, the passenger ship *Phoenix* was destroyed by fire while crossing Lake Michigan. An estimated 250 persons died in the flames. Thirteen years later the passenger steamer *Lady Elgin* was rammed and sunk by a lumber schooner not far from Chicago. The steamer took nearly 300 passengers down with her. The accident took place in September 1860, only a couple of months before the election of President Abraham Lincoln.

While the lakes' lighthouses and their keepers could have done nothing to prevent the tragedies mentioned above, they have saved countless ships, crews, and passengers from what might have been even worse calamities. One way lighthouses save lives is by helping ships and their pilots keep to safe channels.

During the 1860s, while the nation's attention was focused on the Civil War, shipping increased dramatically on Lake Michigan, especially along the 250-mile shoreline of Door County. The Indians called this land "Death's Door" because of the tricky currents and dangerous reefs that claimed the lives of many braves who tried to navigate the channel into Green Bay. White people took a less foreboding view of this region and shortened its name to "Door." Not long after the immigrant influx into Door County began, many lighthouses were built to make the channels less threatening. Today, Door County, Wisconsin, claims more lighthouses than any other county in the United States.

The best way to see and enjoy these lights is to stop first in Sturgeon Bay at the Door County Maritime Museum, located adjacent to Sunset Park at the foot of Florida Street. Curator Gary Soule will be glad to provide directions to all the lights and current information on accessibility.

*Among the most popular Door County lighthouses is that at **Cana Island** (above).*

GRAND TRAVERSE LIGHT
North Port, Michigan – 1853 and 1858

Built before the Civil War, the Grand Traverse Lighthouse served several generations of lake sailors before being decommissioned in 1972. After casting its powerful beacon out across Lake Michigan for well over a century, the old lighthouse was retired, its duties taken over by a simple skeleton structure with relatively little character. But, fortunately for those of us who love historic architecture, the original buildings have been preserved and are exceptionally well maintained.

Established in 1853 to guide shipping in and out of Traverse Bay, the lighthouse was built on Cat's Head Point. Here, with its powerful fourth-order Fresnel lens, it could command the entrance to the bay. The lens beamed out toward the lake from atop a square tower and lantern room rising through the pitched roof of a

Lighthouse architects often combined dwelling and tower, as they did here at Grand Traverse on Lake Michigan. This made the keeper's job a little easier. Located on Cat's Head Point, the light marks the entrance of Grand Traverse Bay.

large, two-story brick dwelling. Even in this isolated location, keepers and their families could live comfortably in the ample dwelling.

The station's first keeper was Philo Beers, who also served as a U.S. deputy marshall. Apparently, the station had need of a lawman. While still under construction in 1852, it was raided by Mormon followers of a self-proclaimed king with the nearly appropriate name of Strang. Not overly literal in their reading of the Ten Commandments, these religious raiders stole everything they could lay their hands on, including some of Beers' lighthouse equipment. Fortunately, the deputy marshall managed to drive off the king's men and save the station's all-important Fresnel lens.

Today the lighthouse is a museum filled with exhibits and mementos offering visitors a glimpse of life in a turn-of-the-century lighthouse. Among its exhibits is the station's original Fresnel lens.

The lantern room at Grand Traverse Lighthouse provides visitors with an extraordinary view.

The Grand Traverse Lighthouse is located in Leelanau State Park at the end of a long peninsula pointing northward on the Lake Michigan side of the Michigan mitten. From Traverse City follow M-22 to Northport. There you take CR-201 and follow the signs to the park. The large, two-story brick dwelling is furnished with antiques, toys, and even dishes on the table, as if the keeper and his family had just stepped outside for a moment. If you've wondered what life was like in a lighthouse, this is a good place to fuel your imagination. The lighthouse museum is open 12:00–5:00 P.M. each day from the last week of June through Labor Day. During September, October, and the first three weeks of June, it is open the same hours but on weekends only.

POINT BETSIE LIGHT
Frankfort, Michigan – 1858

The French called this place "Pointe Aux Becs Scies," or "Sawed Beak Point," but English-speaking settlers gave a less dramatic name: Point Betsie. The government built the Point Betsie Lighthouse in 1858 to mark a key turning place for ships entering or exiting the strategic Manitou Passage. Ever since then lake sailors have considered this one of the most important lights on Lake Michigan. The original thirty-seven-foot tower and attached two-story dwelling (enlarged in 1894) still stand, and the light still burns each night.

The Point Betsie Lighthouse was one of the last lights on the Great Lakes to be automated. Resident keepers operated the light until 1983, when electronic machinery took over for human hands. In fact, coastguardsmen still live in the spacious dwelling. The tower still has its original fourth-order Fresnel lens, too.

For more than a century, Lake Michigan's often angry waters have chopped away at Point Betsie, eroding the beach as if determined to reclaim the land from the keepers and Coast Guard personnel who lived there.

To slow the steadily advancing lake waters and save the structure, the government has erected steel breakwaters and concrete abutments. A broad concrete apron pushes out from the base of the tower to the edge of the lake. The lighthouse now seems stable enough, but in a storm you can feel the walls shake when the waves crash onto the apron.

A private residence, Point Betsie Lighthouse is closed to the public but can be viewed from the roadway. To reach Point Betsie follow M-22 for 5 1/2 miles north from Frankfort, Michigan, and turn left on Point Betsie Road. The road dead-ends at Lake Michigan, a little more than half a mile ahead. The lighthouse is on the right as you approach the lake.

BIG SABLE POINT LIGHT

Ludington, Michigan – 1924

During its early days Ludington, Michigan, had one of the most unusual fog signals in the country. A metal horn made in the shape of a long bugle, it stood beside a train track. Whenever a blanket of fog rolled in from the lake, the citizens of Ludington brought a steam locomotive up to the tongue of the horn and periodically gave a blast on its whistle. Magnified by the horn, the train whistle could be heard for many miles out onto the lake.

Eventually, when lighthouse officials recognized the importance of the area to shipping, the good-hearted people of Ludington were no longer required to rely solely on their ingenuity to protect sailors out on the lake. The construction of the 107-foot-tall Big Sable Point Lighthouse just north of town in 1867 gave ships off

Ludington a worthy navigational aid to guide them along the coast. The lighthouse was fitted with a third-order Fresnel lens, and a fog-signal house was built nearby.

Originally a conical brick structure, the tower had begun to crumble by the turn of the century. To save it lighthouse officials had it encased in steel plates, giving it a ribbed appearance. The plates have done their job well, as the tower has remained solid now for nearly a century. Painted white, it has a broad black middle section to make it more distinctive as a daymark. Surrounded by shifting dunes, Big Sable is one of the more scenic light stations in the country.

For Big Sable Point Lighthouse, take US-10 to Ludington. Turn right onto Lakeshore Drive, follow it for approximately 6 miles, cross the Big Sable River, and enter Ludington State Park. The lighthouse can be reached only via a trail about 1/2 mile in length; but the park is so lovely, you'll be glad of the walk. You can also walk directly up the beach to the lighthouse. For directions stop at the park entrance. For Ludington Pierhead Lighthouse take Ludington Avenue to Stearns Park. The lighthouse stands at the end of a long pier.

LITTLE SABLE POINT LIGHT

Silver Lake State Park, Michigan – 1874

When completed in 1874 the lighthouse tower at Little Sable Point was nearly a twin of its sister at Big Sable Point near Ludington. Both towers stood 107 feet tall, both were constructed of brick, and both had a third-order Fresnel lens.

The Big Sable Point tower deteriorated and was eventually covered with steel plates, but the tower at Little Sable Point still looks much as it did 120 years ago. The keeper's dwelling, however, was demolished during the 1950s when the lighthouse was automated, leaving the tower to stand a solitary vigil. One of the loveliest lighthouse towers on the lakes, its red-brick walls offer a handsome contrast to the white dunes and the blue water of the lake beyond.

From US-31 a few miles south of the town of Mears, turn west onto Shelby Road. After about 3 1/2 miles, turn right on Scenic Drive, right on Buchanan Avenue, left on 18th Avenue, and left again onto Silver Lake Road. In Silver Lake State Park you'll find a parking area near Lake Michigan and Little Sable Point Lighthouse.

For the White River Lighthouse turn west from US-31 onto White Lake Road (near the town of Whitehall), then left on South Shore Road and right onto Murray Road. The museum here has the station's original fourth-order Fresnel lens on display.

Little Sable Lighthouse stands its solitary vigil.
(Courtesy John W. Weil)

MICHIGAN CITY LIGHT

Michigan City, Indiana – 1858

Just as Kansas City, Missouri, is not in Kansas, Michigan City is not in Michigan. It is in Indiana on the Lake Michigan shore a few dozen miles to the west of South Bend. Long an important shipping point, the Michigan City Harbor has been served by a lighthouse since 1837.

The city's first lighthouse, a simple brick-and-stone tower, was replaced by a more elaborate structure in 1858. Built with wood and brick at a cost of $8,000, it had a large central gable and a squat tower and lantern room perched on the roof. Today the old Michigan City Lighthouse looks more like a schoolhouse or library than a navigational aid. Indeed, it has been out of service since 1904, when it was replaced by a nearby pier light and converted into a residence. Eventually, the Coast Guard abandoned the building, handing it over to the Michigan City Historical Society for use as a lighthouse museum.

Out of service since 1904, the Michigan City Lighthouse is now a museum.

MICHIGAN CITY EAST PIER LIGHT
Michigan City, Indiana – 1904

The Michigan City East Pier Lighthouse has guided ships in and out of the harbor since the early twentieth century. Built on a square concrete platform, the structure has a pyramidal roof. An octagonal tower thrusts through the roof, raising the focal plane of the light more than fifty feet above the lake. Like many similar pier lighthouses, this one is encased in steel to protect it from storms.

During the tremendous storm of November 1913, the keeper of the East Pier Lighthouse took refuge on the mainland throughout most of the heavy weather. For three days the waves pounded the pier and the lighthouse. When it was all over, about 200 feet of the elevated walkway connecting the lighthouse with the mainland had been destroyed. To enable the keeper to reach the lighthouse, engineers rigged up an aerial tram with a breeches buoy (a life preserver with a pantslike canvas seat). Keepers used this rather adventurous system for several months until the elevated walkway was repaired.

It is said that, during the 1920s, keeper Ralph Moore hurried his three daughters inside whenever he saw a certain speedboat roaring through the channel. "Get . . . in the house," Moore would shout. "That damn fool is coming." The particular "damn fool" the keeper had in mind was none other than Al Capone, the Chicago gangster. Capone had a house on nearby Long Beach and reached it by boat rather than drive and take a chance on being ambushed by rival bad guys.

Located in Washington Park off Heisman Harbor Road, the Michigan City Lighthouse is now a delightful museum. Open from noon until 4:00 P.M., it contains many interesting exhibits, including the station's fifth-order Fresnel lens, hand-crafted in Paris around the turn of the century. A great place to watch sunsets from the beach. Follow US-35 to US-12 and Pine Street (one-way), then go over a bridge into Washington Park. The lighthouse is across from the Naval Armory building and has its own parking area. To reach the Michigan City East Pier Lighthouse, drive around the park to the beach parking area (there's a small parking fee here).

Connected to the mainland by a catwalk, the Michigan City East Pier Lighthouse took over from its sister lighthouse on shore in 1904. In heavy weather, the catwalk provided the only safe access to the tower. During the 1920s, gangster Al Capone often raced past this tower in his speedboat.

CHICAGO HARBOR LIGHT

Chicago, Illinois – 1832 and 1893

The first Chicago lighthouse, one of the earliest on the Great Lakes, was built at the mouth of the Chicago River in 1832. As Chicago grew into one of the Earth's greatest cities, a series of lights, built both on the mainland and on piers in the harbor, guided a tremendous volume of shipping traffic in and out of the city. Because the St. Lawrence Seaway makes Chicago a seaport and not just a lakeport, ships from every maritime nation have docked here.

The Harbor Lighthouse seen today originally stood on the mainland, at the entrance of the Chicago River, near the site of the city's first lighthouse. Built in 1893, it was given an especially fine third-order Fresnel lens, which had been intended for the Point Loma Lighthouse in California. The lens had been placed on display at Chicago's Columbian Exposition. When this now-legendary world's fair was over, lighthouse officials decided to place the lens in the recently completed Harbor Lighthouse.

In 1917, just before the United States entered World War I, the lighthouse was moved to the end of a harbor breakwater. There it has remained. Each night its historic lens throws its light out across the harbor from the lantern room atop the forty-eight-foot brick-and-steel tower.

The lighthouse is closed to the public but can be seen from many points along the Chicago waterfront.

From Lake Michigan the first spire in Chicago's well-known skyline is that of the Chicago Harbor Lighthouse. The old tower has an especially fine Fresnel lens, which was once on display at the city's Columbian Exposition.

GROSSE POINT LIGHT

Evanston, Illinois – 1873

Among the most beautiful and storied lights on the Great Lakes, the Grosse Point Lighthouse is in many ways a superlative structure. Its second-order Fresnel is one of the most powerful lenses on the lakes, while its 113-foot tower is one of the tallest. The conical brick tower, painted yellow and trimmed in red, is exceptionally graceful.

A powerful, second-order Fresnel beams into a purple evening sky at Grosse Point Lighthouse. (Courtesy Donald J. Terras)

Although it was decommissioned by the Coast Guard in 1935 and operates today as a private navigational aide, the Grosse Point Lighthouse continues to serve lake sailors just as it has since 1873. Built during the early 1870s for approximately $50,000, the station was meant to serve as a primary coastal light. It was given a double-sized keepers' dwelling and several outbuildings, which housed the fog signal and other equipment. The brick of the tower deteriorated over the years, and in 1914 the tower was encased in a layer of concrete.

Today the lighthouse stands on a street lined with fine old lakefront homes. Northwestern University is nearby. The lighthouse grounds and some of its buildings are used as a nature center and a maritime center, both open to the public on weekends during the summer.

Take I–94 north out of Chicago or south from Milwaukee to the Old Orchard exit. Drive east toward Evanston until Old Orchard ends. Then turn left, go 2 blocks, and turn right onto Central Street. Follow Central about 4 miles until it ends at the lighthouse, which is located adjacent to Northwestern University on Sheridan Road in Evanston. The grounds are open to the public daily. Graced by stately trees almost as tall as the tower itself, the setting makes this one of the most attractive light stations on the Great Lakes. The yellow tower matches the brick of the keeper's residence. For current information call (708) 328–6961.

CHAPTER FIVE

LIGHTS OF
THE LEVIATHAN LAKE

Superior

Two lighthouses are reflected in the window of a keeper's dwelling on Michigan Island in Wisconsin's Apostle Islands. The iron-skeleton tower is still in use. The much older, and shorter, stone tower can be seen at the left.

Lights of the Leviathan Lake

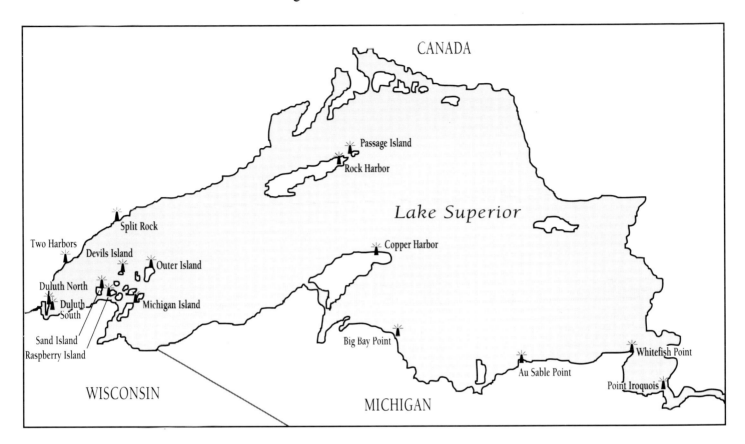

Sand Island juts out into the vastness of Lake Superior. It is one of more than twenty islands in the Apostles, named by the French who believed there were only twelve isles here. Today the Apostle Islands invite national lakeshore visitors to enjoy an unsurpassed selection of historical lighthouses.

K nown to Native Americans as Gitche Gumee and to most others as Superior, it is the Earth's greatest freshwater lake. More than 350 miles long, 160 miles wide, and a quarter of a mile deep, it covers 31,200 square miles of the continental heartland in a cold, dark blanket of blue water. A liquid highway for ore, grain, and chemical freighters, container ships, and vessels of every description, it is one of the most heavily traveled bodies of water on the planet. Yet its shores include some of the most isolated spots in North America.

The lighthouse keepers who once served at Lake Superior's remote outposts, places like Rock of Ages, Passage Island, and Au Sable, were surely among the loneliest men and women in America, and the toughest. Usually located at water's edge, lighthouses and their keepers are often no less exposed to heavy weather than the ships and sailors they serve. But, unlike ships, lighthouses cannot move, cannot run for safe harbor, cannot remain tied up at the dock until the worst is over. In a storm they must stand their ground and take their beating, and so must their keepers.

During the 1960s and 1970s, the Coast Guard automated the last manned lighthouses on the Great Lakes, including those on Superior. Afterward, their lamps and mechanisms operated by computers, photosensitive cells, and other electronic "keepers," the lake lighthouses continued their vigil alone. Always in the past, however, their work had required the help of human hands.

LIFE ON THE ROCKS

It is easy to imagine that lighthouse keepers were hermits, fugitives from noisy city streets and crowded factories who preferred a simpler more peaceful life at water's edge. Generally speaking, however, that was not the case. Mostly they were ordinary Americans glad of the steady work and regular pay.

Keepers' salaries never amounted to much, often no more than $50.00 per month and much less than that during the nineteenth century; but, almost by definition, the job came with a house and an excellent view. Remote light stations were supplied with food, delivered every few months by government lighthouse tenders, and usually there was a plot of ground where the keepers could grow vegetables and raise a few chickens. Many keepers lived with their families; but some stations, such as the Rock of Ages Lighthouse, were much too isolated or too dangerous for family life.

Looking something like an enormous spark plug, the Rock of Ages Lighthouse rises from the open waters of Lake Superior about five miles off Isle Royale, itself one of the nation's most remote places. Nowadays, like all other Great Lakes lighthouses, the Rock of Ages Light is automated. But from 1908, the year it went into service, until the last resident crew left the station in 1977, the light was operated by a keeper and three assistants, who would remain on "the Rock" for up to eight months at a time. They arrived at the station in April and were taken ashore again in early December, when the thickening ice forced shipping off the lakes. The denizens of the Rock were allowed occasional shore leave on Isle Royale, but otherwise they lived at the station full-time. In heavy weather no one could approach the station or leave it. If radio communication went down, the station crew could be cut off from all contact with the outside world.

Utterly barren, the Rock itself was only about fifty feet wide and supported not a single bush or blade of grass. Inside the 130-foot steelplated tower, a spiral staircase offered access to a few small bunk rooms where the keepers slept; a galley and dining area where they ate; storage and equipment rooms where they worked; and, of course, the lantern room, with its huge second-order Fresnel lens. For the most part this was the keepers' whole world.

In 1931, in the midst of the Great Depression, a young Detroit reporter named Stella Champney sailed with the tender *Marigold* as it made its semiannual visits to Lake Superior lighthouses. At the Rock of Ages Lighthouse, she interviewed first assistant keeper C. A. McKay.

Only the year before McKay had had a terrifying experience. As a storm brewed out on the lake, his boss, keeper Emil Mueller, had fallen from the tower's spiral staircase and landed squarely on the bed where McKay was sleeping. McKay was uninjured, but Mueller lay dead of a heart attack.

McKay's explanation for the tragic incident was a simple one: "Too many steps. One room on top of another clear to the top. His heart gave out."

This rare photograph (perhaps the only one existing) shows the lighthouse tender Marigold *making another of its appointed rounds. Named for flowers and plants, the tenders brought food, supplies, mail, and welcome human contact to keepers at isolated Great Lakes light stations.* (Courtesy Anna Hoge)

The wreck of *Edmund Fitzgerald* was neither the worst shipping loss nor the most mysterious disappearance on the Great Lakes. Superior has swallowed many ships. So have the other lakes. But the *Fitzgerald* has become a popular and poignant symbol for all such calamities.

In 1980 celebrated undersea explorer Jacques Cousteau sent his famous ship *Calypso* in search of the *Fitzgerald*. The *Calypso*'s sonar located the wreck some 500 feet down, and an eager team of divers splashed into the water. The divers found a dented and misshapen hull broken into two sections. The damage they saw convinced them that the ship had broken apart on the surface. They felt the bow and stern halves might have floated on the surface for a while before sinking. Unfortunately, Superior's ice-cold water allowed the divers only a few minutes to examine the wreck.

A more careful study of the wreckage had to await the arrival of sophisticated computer technology. During the mid-1980s computer-guided, free-swimming robots (Remote Operated Vehicles, or ROVs) made visits to the *Titanic*, the *Bismarck*, and other well-known wrecks. Oblivious to the cold, dark, and crushing pressures at extreme depths, the tireless robots could stay below for hours. In 1989 a research expedition including experts from the National Geographic Society, the U.S. Fish and Wildlife Service, the Great Lakes Shipwreck Historical Society, and several other organizations employed an ROV to investigate the wreck of the *Edmund Fitzgerald*. Gliding silently through an eerie world as separate from our own as the surface of the moon or Mars, the ROV turned its lights and television cameras onto the battered *Fitz*.

The data collected by the ROV led the investigators to conclude the *Calypso*'s divers had been mistaken. Pieces of the ship had been twisted, bent, and stretched by the force of the water as the *Fitzgerald* raced, bow first, toward the bottom. Apparently, the ship had not broken up on the surface but had perished in a sudden, cataclysmic plunge into the lake's depths.

Still, many questions remained. The most tantalizing of them: What became of the crew? Seeking answers, the ROV headed for the *Fitzgerald*'s bridge. As the ROV worked its way carefully through the wreckage and into the pilot house, a hush fell over the scientists on the research vessel *Grayling* way up above on the surface. What would the ROV discover?

Inside the pilot house the ROV trained its cameras on limp microphone cables, tangled bundles of wire, a fallen water cooler, a smashed radar console, and other shattered equipment. But there were no clues here to the fate of the crew. Except, perhaps, for one. The port side door swung limply on its hinges. It had been left open.

Did Captain McSorley and the other men in the pilot house escape through that open door? Did he and his crew consign themselves to the mercy of the waves only to be overwhelmed by the storm? We will never know for sure what happened to them, but guided by the light of our imaginations we can reconstruct the final moments of the *Fitzgerald* crew.

As the last waves struck the ship, most of the men had been ordered below decks to keep them out of harm's way. To pass the time, ease the tension, and take their minds off the war that nature had declared on them and their ship, they told jokes and laughed nervously. There were stories told of other storms on other lakes, of adventures on the high seas. Some sailors' tales have roots so deep in marine tradition they reach all the way back to the time of the Roman grain ships and before that to the age of Ulysses. The poetic memories of mariners are as ageless as the dangers they face.

Unaware that they stood on the brink of eternity, the crew of the *Fitzgerald* shared the bond that has always made brothers of sailors, and, for that matter, of lighthouse keepers. They were men caught in the grip of a hostile sea. And, as loyal sailors have always done, they counted on the keen seamanship of their captain, and a bit of luck, to pull them through.

This time their captain was not lucky. Neither were they. A shudder ran through the ship. They could feel the shudder, and hear it, while up on the bridge their captain stood peering into the darkness, searching the distance for a light.

Like spear points, limestone cliffs threaten any sailor who dares approach Devils Island in the Apostles. Because of the booming noise made by waves striking the cliffs and rushing into the caves between, Indians considered this place evil.

Both **Big Bay Point Lighthouse** *(1896) and* **Point Iroquois Lighthouse** *(1871) once guarded especially dangerous stretches of Michigan shoreline where many ships have been lost. Deactivated in 1961, Big Bay Point is now a charming bed and breakfast. Guests are welcome to climb the spiral staircase inside the five-story tower to enjoy one of the finest views in Michigan. For information call (906) 345–9957 or write Big Bay Point Lighthouse, #3 Lighthouse Road, Big Bay, MI 49808. Point Iroquois (right) ended its service in 1965; but its impressive sixty-five-foot brick tower now houses a museum and gift shop. On sale is* Lighthouse Memories: Growing up at Point Iroquois, *a memoir by Betty Byrnes Bacon. For more information call (906) 437–5272.*

WHITEFISH POINT LIGHT
Whitefish Point, Michigan – 1848 and 1861

The southeastern reaches of Lake Superior have long been known as a grave-yard for ships. Hundreds of vessels, including the famed *Edmund Fitzgerald*, lay on the cold, deep bottom here where the lake approaches Whitefish Bay. The loss of so many ships in this area is made all the more bitter, and mysterious, by the fact that the bay itself is relatively calm. Seemingly, even in the worst of storms, the ships and their crews only need to round Whitefish Point to reach safety. But all too often they have failed to do either.

The very first ship known to sail on Superior, the sixty-foot trading vessel *Invincible*, perished in gale-force winds and towering waves near here in 1816. Many other vessels have suffered the same fate. Some were big, well-known ships such as the *Edmund Fitzgerald,* and their destruction made headlines across the country. Many others were lesser vessels, but their loss was nonetheless tragic.

In 1915 the 186-foot lumber freighter *Myron* foundered in a blizzard off White-fish Point. The weight of the ice building up on the hull and deck dragged the freighter farther and farther down into the waves until water, pouring into the holds, snuffed out the fires in the boiler room. With no power, the little ship was doomed. The crew managed to scramble into lifeboats, but the water around the ship was filled with tons of lumber that had washed overboard. Thrown about like battering rams by the waves, the heavy lumber crushed the lifeboat and the men in them. The keeper and his family at Whitefish Point Light Station could hear the

A layer of fog cloaks Whitefish Point in a shroud of mystery.

prayers and screams of the sailors as they died but could do nothing to help. Ironically, the captain, who had elected to go down with his ship, survived by clinging to a piece of the shattered pilothouse until it washed up on the beach.

Probably the smallest wreck ever on Lake Superior involved no ships at all, only a surfboat and two stranded fishermen. One afternoon in April 1933, a pair of Michigan sportsmen were very unhappily surprised to discover that the field of ice where they were fishing had broken away from the mainland and drifted out onto the open lake. A Coast Guard surfboat raced out across the lake to rescue the hapless anglers. Unfortunately, the boat was caught and crushed between two massive blocks of groaning ice, leaving three coastguardsmen marooned along with the fishermen. Eventually, the keeper of Whitefish Point Light Station managed to reach the stranded men and bring them back to the lighthouse. There, no doubt, they were treated to a hot bath and warm meal.

When the November winds blow on Lake Superior, the most welcome sight a sailor is likely to see is the beacon from the Whitefish Point Lighthouse. This light has shined onto the big lake more or less unfailingly—except for the night when the *Fitzgerald* went down—for almost 150 years. To many lake sailors the light is more than a navigational marker—it is a welcoming call from home.

The Whitefish Point Lighthouse is a remarkable structure. A steel cylinder some eighty feet tall, it is supported by a skeletal steel framework. Its modern, functional appearance is all the more extraordinary when one considers that it was built in 1861, during Abraham Lincoln's first year in the White House. Lighthouse engineers were experimenting with skeletal structures at that time. The design is intended to take stress off the building during high winds.

Storms were not the only dangers faced by lighthouses and their keepers. In February 1925 the keeper at Whitefish Bay sent this wire to officials in Detroit: "I have respectfully to report an earthquake shock being felt at this station at 8:25 last night. The shock was in the nature of a rocking and rolling and was so pronounced that the dwelling could be seen moving forth and back in an east-west direction and the window curtains swung in and out about four to six inches. Even the rocking chair in which this writer was sitting was arrested in its motion by the twisting of the dwelling. I have examined the station today, the tower in particular, and am happy to say that I can find no damage done to the lens, lantern, or the tower itself."

Automated by the Coast Guard in 1970, the station no longer has a resident keeper. Appropriately, the dwelling now houses the Great Lakes Shipwreck Museum. Here visitors with open eyes and active imaginations can step back in time and relive the last moments aboard the *Fitzgerald* and many other unlucky ships claimed forever by the lakes.

One of America's most fabled light stations, the Whitefish Point Lighthouse can be reached from Mackinac Bridge by taking I–75 north to M-123 to Paradise. From Paradise follow Wire Road to the point. A worthwhile additional attraction is the Great Lakes Shipwreck Museum, where the haunting world of shipwrecks can be explored. The museum is open from 10:00 A.M. to 6:00 P.M. every day from Memorial Day through the middle of October.

AU SABLE POINT LIGHT

Grand Marais, Michigan – 1874

On the night of August 21, 1930, sailors aboard the lighthouse tender *Amaranth* were astonished by a mysterious beam of light cutting through the night air directly over their ship. The *Amaranth* was under way in Lake Superior about eighteen miles due west of Au Sable Point in Michigan. Barely clearing the tender's highest spars, the beam seemed about 100 feet wide and located directly over the ship. The light remained over the *Amaranth* for about an hour and then vanished as suddenly as it had appeared. The captain and crew of the tender were quite certain that what they saw was not an errant beam from a nearby lighthouse. Nor was it a display of the northern lights. Or so they reported to Lighthouse Service officials in Detroit. The strange light was never seen again and the mystery of its appearance was never cleared up.

The lighthouse tender Amaranth *and its sister ships were the sole means of sustenance for many a grateful lighthouse keeper.* (Courtesy U.S. Coast Guard)

There are many unsolved mysteries in this part of Superior. The beaches of Michigan's Upper Peninsula are strewn with carcasses of ships large and small. What happened to these vessels? What became of their crews? Often the answers to those questions lie locked away in the lake.

For many years sailors dreaded the eighty miles of dark shoreline that stretched eastward from Grand Island Lighthouse to the famed light on Whitefish Point. Unmarked by any navigational light, these dangerous shores claimed dozens of ships. To fill the gap and save lives, a lighthouse was placed on Au Sable Point in 1874.

An eighty-seven-foot brick tower was built on a rise, placing the light about 107 feet above the lake surface. Its third-order Fresnel lens displayed a fixed white light. The attached, two-story brick keeper's dwelling was spacious, but those who lived in it knew theirs was one of the most remote mainland light stations in America. The nearest town, Grand Marais, was more than a dozen miles away, and there was no road. Keepers either hiked in or came by boat.

Perhaps because of its isolation, the Coast Guard automated the light in 1958, turning the property and buildings over to the National Park Service for inclusion in Pictured Rocks National Lakeshore. Although the light remains active, the old

Fresnel lens has been removed and placed in the Nautical and Maritime Museum in Grand Marais.

Pictured Rocks National Lakeshore encompasses a remarkable variety of attractions, including Munsing Falls, Miners Castle (a nine story-tall monolith), trails, streams, woodlands, beaches, and, of course, Au Sable Light Station. Twelve miles of beach offer solitude and nearly endless barefoot walks over white sand and pebbles. Grand Sable Dunes cannot match the Sahara for sheer size, but its four square miles of shifting sand are enough to impress.

Among the least accessible mainland light stations in the United States is Au Sable Point Lighthouse, shown here on a sunny summer afternoon. There has never been an all-weather road; and even today, visitors must walk in or reach the lighthouse by means of an often treacherous dirt-and-gravel access road.

Just as its keepers once did, visitors today must walk to this lighthouse, which is located in Pictured Rocks National Lakeshore on the Upper Peninsula. From Highway 28 take Highway 77 north about 25 miles to Grand Marais. The lighthouse is a considerable distance from the park headquarters in Grand Marais. To reach it, take Alger County Road (H-58), a dirt and gravel access road, for about 12 miles. The Hurricane River Campground provides access to a trail leading to the lighthouse and the lake. During the summer months a ranger is on duty at the keeper's house and conducts a three-hour walk called "Shipwrecks and Lighthouses." For more information call the National Park Service at (906) 387–2607 or write Pictured Rocks National Lakeshore, P.O. Box 40, Munsing, MI 49862.

The National Park Service has established a maritime museum in a Coast Guard building in Grand Marais. Even the museum's restrooms are historic. During the November 1975 storm that sank the Edmund Fitzgerald, the last radio contact with the ship was from the communications room in this building. That room has been subdivided into men's and women's lavatories. A sign in each restroom says, "You are now seated in almost the same spot where the last message from the Fitzgerald was received."

COPPER HARBOR LIGHT

Copper Harbor, Michigan – 1849 and 1867

The fresh water of the Great Lakes freezes more easily than the salty ocean. Beginning usually about the middle of December, winter temperatures in the frigid upper Midwest turn lake surfaces as hard as slate. For this reason the ice-locked lakes are closed to navigation for several months each year. In the days before lighthouses were automated, keepers on the Keweenaw Peninsula and elsewhere on Lake Superior typically shut down their lights for the winter and moved to some safer and warmer place. When winter came early and hit hard, it could make the journey very difficult indeed.

On December 16, 1925, Copper Harbor Range Light keeper Charles Davis loaded his family and belongings onto a mule-drawn wagon and prepared to move them into a nearby town. Just before he left a letter arrived from the superintendent of lighthouses, ordering Davis to keep his light burning for another three days. There were still freighters out on the lake. Like most keepers, Davis took his duties

Ferry passengers can get this close-up view of Copper Harbor Light Station.

very seriously. He sent his wife and family on ahead and remained behind himself to tend the light. That evening a blizzard set in and Davis had to wear snowshoes to walk from the keeper's dwelling to his light tower. The following is excerpted from his report on the experience.

"The snow was deep and soft. The snowshoes would sink about a foot and load up with snow at every step. I was panting like a hound before . . . I reached the main light. I had it flashing at 7:05. It took me until 8:10 to get back here. Mr. Bergh [a friend from a nearby village] had a fire started when I got back, which was a blessing as I was wringing wet with perspiration and too tired to eat, sleep, or move."

Winters on Michigan's Upper Peninsula are notoriously severe. But the weather did not deter the rapid development of mining when deposits of copper were found during the 1840s and then iron later in the century. The richest veins of copper were located on the Keweenaw Peninsula, which thrusts out to the northeast toward the center of Lake Superior. Ship traffic in and out of Copper Harbor and nearby Eagle Harbor expanded rapidly to carry the copper bounty to markets in the east. As a result government officials soon saw the need for lighthouses at both locations.

The first Copper Harbor lighthouse was completed in 1849. A stone tower with a detached dwelling, it was located on a point near the harbor entrance. Upgraded and given a Fresnel lens in 1856, it was replaced with an entirely new structure shortly after the Civil War. A square stone tower with a small attached dwelling, this second Copper Harbor Lighthouse still stands, although its duties have been taken over by a nearby skeleton tower. Copper Harbor also has a pair of range lights marking the shipping channel. The wooden rear range lighthouse dates to 1869.

Since there is no public road, the Copper Harbor Lighthouse can be reached only by water. Chartered boats are available at the Municipal Marina, just off Michigan Route 26 in Copper Harbor. For information call (906) 289–4215. The 15-minute boat ride to the light is pleasant, and the lovely setting of the brick tower and dwelling are well worth the trip. Inside the dwelling is a small museum, and nearby is one of the area's first copper mines, now properly fenced off to prevent accidents. To reach the Eagle Harbor Lighthouse, follow MI-26 down the Keneewaw Peninsula. Turn left toward the lake just before entering the town of Eagle Harbor.

LIGHTHOUSES OF THE APOSTLE ISLANDS

Michigan Island – 1857 and 1869

Raspberry Island – 1863

Sand Island – 1881

Devils Island – 1891 and 1901

As anyone who has seen them is likely to agree, the Apostle Islands off Wisconsin's Chequamegon Peninsula are truly a national treasure. Widely appreciated for its natural beauty, wildlife, and pristine beaches, the Apostle Islands National Lakeshore offers another extraordinary attraction: an elegant, jeweled necklace of six old lighthouses. Well maintained by the National Park Service, these venerable structures make the Apostle Islands something of an outdoor lighthouse museum.

Built in 1857, Michigan Island Lighthouse is the oldest in the Apostles. The whitewashed stucco tower and dwelling suggest a New England coastal lighthouse. This light guided ships along the eastern side of the Apostles for more than seventy years before its duties were taken over by a skeleton-style light tower still in operation today.

Built on a high bank, the wood-frame tower of the Raspberry Island Lighthouse dates to the Civil War. Until 1957 its fifth-order lens shined from the lantern room in the forty-foot-tall tower.

Nearby Outer Island Lighthouse went into service in 1874. A traditional conical brick tower some eighty feet tall, it stands on a high bank raising the focal plane of its third-order Fresnel more than 130 feet above the lake surface.

On the west side of the Apostles, Sand Island Lighthouse guided ships for half

The Devils Island Fresnel witnessed the frigid winter of 1924-25, when its keeper had to service a gas-powered buoy in frozen Chequamegon Bay by dogsled.

In 1957, the Coast Guard removed Raspberry Island's light and mounted it on a pole in front of the fog-signal building.

a century (1881 to 1931) before it, too, was replaced by a steel skeleton tower. The original brownstone structure was afterward leased as a private residence, and it has survived the years since intact.

Devils Island has little in common with the infamous French penal colony of the same name. Keepers lived quite comfortably in its spacious Queen Anne–style brick dwelling. The station was so well appointed, in fact, that it attracted a visit from President and Mrs. Calvin Coolidge in August 1928. Accompanied by a party of about fifty well-wishers, the fun-loving Coolidge enjoyed a sumptuous lunch on the station dock. Such events were rare, to say the least, and are no longer seen in the Apostles. Devils Island Lighthouse, placed in operation in 1881, was the last of the Apostle Islands lights to be automated. Electronic timers and other machinery took over from the last human keepers in 1978.

First visit the Apostle Islands National Lakeshore headquarters, in the old county court-house building in Bayfield. Here you can enjoy an antique Fresnel lens, learn about the islands from the various interpretive exhibits, and pick up information on visiting the islands. To plan your tour write National Lakeshore Headquarters, Chief of Interpretation, Route 1 Box 4, Bayfield, WI 54814.

The Apostle Islands Cruise Service offers a number of island trips including an Inner Island Shuttle to Sand Island with a 2-mile hike to the lighthouse there. Some trips visit Raspberry Island and other islands, although these may not put you within reach of a light-house. For cruise information call (715) 779 3925 or 779–5153.

Although it cannot be seen from either the Upper or Lower peninsula, the state of Michigan contains one of North America's most remarkable land forms. A giant island (seventy miles long) completely surrounded by the azure waters of Lake Superior, it is as remote as it is magnificent. Luckily for those of us who value wilderness and natural beauty, all of Isle Royale's 209 square miles are now protected by a national park.

Today Isle Royale has the feeling of a pristine wilderness; but, surprisingly, the island was once an active mining center. The discovery of copper here during the late 1840s led to construction of the **Rock Harbor Lighthouse** (above) to guide ore freighters to the island. The station included a fifty-foot brick tower with an attached stone dwelling. The Isle Royale copper veins were exhausted within a few years, and by the late 1870s mining activity had ceased altogether. This made the Rock Harbor Light unnecessary, and it was closed permanently in 1879. The tower and dwelling still stand.

Off the northern end of Isle Royale is Passage Island. Since 1882 the channel between the two islands has been marked by the **Passage Island Light.** Built up on a cliff at the north end of the thickly forested island, the old stone lighthouse looks out into the channel. From a distance it could be taken for a church. For more than one sailor caught in a storm, its beacon, visible from twenty-five miles away, has been the answer to prayers. (Both photos courtesy of Bob and Sandra Shanklin)

The lighthouses on or near Isle Royale can be reached only by boat or seaplane. For information on transportation and facilities, write Isle Royale National Park, 87 North Ripley Street, Houghton, MI 49931 or call (906) 482–0984.

LIGHTHOUSES OF THE DULUTH BREAKWATER

South Breakwater Lighthouses – 1901

North Breakwater Lighthouse – 1910

At the far western angle of Lake Superior is Duluth, Minnesota, a hard-working city famous for having provided much of the iron ore fed into the Bessemer furnaces of America's steel mills. Mountains of ore have been loaded here into long Great Lakes freighters for the sometimes dangerous trip to Soo Locks and beyond. Today, in addition to freighters, the Duluth lakefront is attracting throngs of tourists.

Located in the midst of one of the nation's busiest industrial waterfronts, Canal Park offers plenty for visitors to see and enjoy. In addition to the heavily trafficked ship canal, an extraordinary aerial bridge, and a fine maritime museum, there are three delightful lighthouses, each with its own still-operational Fresnel lens.

Built just after the turn of the century, the lighthouses are located on breakwaters

alongside the channel connecting the inner harbor to Lake Superior. A lighthouse was placed beside the channel as early as 1873; but in 1901 it was replaced by a pair of light towers, one at either end of the breakwater. The South Breakwater Outer Lighthouse consists of a thirty-five-foot tower rising from the corner of a squat brick fog-signal building. Its fourth-order Fresnel lens was imported from France. Erected at the same time was the South Breakwater Inner Lighthouse, a steel cylinder–type tower with a supporting skeleton frame. This lighthouse displays a flashing light produced by a fourth-order bull's-eye Fresnel lens.

The Duluth North Breakwater Lighthouse went into service during the spring of 1910. Its metal frame is enclosed by riveted steel plates. The lantern atop its thirty-seven-foot tower contains a fifth-order Fresnel lens.

From I–35 take the Highway 61 exit and follow signs to the waterfront area and Canal Park. The park is right beside the famous Aerial Bridge, only a few blocks from downtown Duluth. The lighthouses are located on piers beside the ship canal. Adjacent to the canal and near the bridge is Canal Park Maritime Museum. Operated by the Army Corps of Engineers, this museum is one of the most visited attractions in Minnesota. The Duluth waterfront centers on Canal Park and is filled with busy shops and restaurants. For more information call (218) 722–4011.

SPLIT ROCK LIGHT
Two Harbors, Minnesota – 1910

Compasses do not always read true in western Lake Superior. Captains steaming toward Duluth are used to seeing their compass needles swing this way and that as if the Earth's magnetic poles had decided to take a holiday. The problem is iron—mountains of it ashore and lesser mountains in the holds of passing ships. In these parts sailors are particularly thankful for lighthouses and other navigational aids.

High up on a Minnesota cliff overlooking Lake Superior stands one of the world's great lighthouses. Photographed literally millions of times, framed in countless postcards, and featured on the covers of hundreds of publications, it may be America's best known and most visited lighthouse.

Ironically, Minnesota's Split Rock Lighthouse is no longer an official Coast Guard light station. But that does not deter the visitors who swarm here every day during the summer to enjoy this magnificent lighthouse and the spectacular view from its high, stony perch.

An octagonal yellow-brick structure, the tower is only fifty-four feet high, but the cliff beneath it soars more than 120 feet over the lake. This places the focal plane of the light 168 feet above the lake level and makes Split Rock one of the loftiest lighthouses on the Great Lakes.

Built in 1910, the lighthouse owes its existence in part to a hurricanelike November blizzard that tore across Superior five years earlier. The great Storm of 1905 caught dozens of ore boats and freighters out on the lake. More than thirty were driven onto rocks and crushed. Several disappeared forever into the lake's extreme depths. One, the 430-foot *Mataafa,* met its end within sight of Duluth Harbor. Another, the *William Edenborn*, was flung ashore and torn apart on Split Rock itself. Dozens of lives were lost in the storm.

The calamity convinced lighthouse officials that navigational aids on Lake Superior must be improved. The most important step they took to accomplish the upgrading was construction of a light station at Split Rock. Building the lighthouse proved a difficult and expensive task. Since there was no road, materials had to be shipped in and lifted to the top of the cliff, using

A storm brews over the Split Rock Lighthouse. Mariners once looked to its powerful light for guidance in foul weather, but no more. Today this magnificent lighthouse is a popular tourist attraction.

a steam hoist. By the time the tower, lantern, fog-signal building, and detached dwellings were completed and the lamps ready to be lit, during the summer of 1910, the project had cost taxpayers more than $72,000.

The station's flashing light was produced by a bivalve–style Fresnel lens that looked something like a huge glass clamshell. For many years light for the beacon came from an oil vapor lamp; but after electricity reached the station in 1939, a 1,000-watt bulb was placed inside the lens. The light flashed once every ten seconds and could be seen from twenty-two miles out on the lake.

The fog signal was powered by gasoline or diesel compressors. Every twenty seconds during fog or heavy weather it gave a deafening blast that could be heard from about five miles away.

The Coast Guard decommissioned the lighthouse in 1969, handing it over to the state of Minnesota for use as a park. More than 200,000 visitors enjoy the lighthouse and surrounding 100-acre park each year. There are several fine trails, and a variety of films and exhibits illuminate the station and its history.

Except for the square tower and lantern, this red-brick structure might fit in well on some old-fashioned residential street. Despite its appearance, Two Harbors Lighthouse remains a hard-working navigational aid. Built to guide huge ore ships in and out of the nearby harbor, it still assists commercial traffic on the lake.

Most travelers reach Split Rock from Duluth or Two Harbors via U.S. 61, otherwise known as the North Shore Highway. The park offers camping and picnicking facilities as well as trails for hiking and crosscountry skiing. Accessible year-round, the park is open daily 8:00 A.M.–10:30 P.M. from May 15 through October 15 and 8:00 A.M.–4:00 P.M. during the rest of the year. The lighthouse, fog-signal building, keeper's dwelling, and a history center are open 9:00 A.M.–5 P.M. from May 15 through October 15. The history center remains open the rest of the year, with hours from noon until 4:00 P.M. on weekends only.

For Two Harbors Lighthouse take US-61 to the town of Two Harbors and follow signs to the harbor area and depot, where parking is available. The lighthouse sits on a nearby hillside.

BIBLIOGRAPHY

Adams, William Henry Davenport. *Lighthouses and Lightships: A Descriptive and Historical Account of Their Mode of Construction and Organization.* New York: Scribner's, 1870.

Adamson, Hans Christian. *Keepers of the Light.* New York: Greenberg, 1955.

Beaver, Patrick. *A History of Lighthouses.* Secaucus, N.J.: Citadel, 1972.

Bowen, Dana Thomas. *Shipwrecks of the Lakes.* Cleveland, Ohio: Freshwater Press, 1952.

Chase, Mary Ellen. *The Story of Lighthouses.* New York: Norton, 1965.

Havighurst, Walter. *The Great Lakes Reader.* New York: Macmillan, 1966.

Heming, Robert. *Ships Gone Missing: The Great Lakes Storm of 1913.* Chicago: Contemporary Books, 1992.

Holland, Francis Ross, Jr. *America's Lighthouses: Their Illustrated History Since 1716.* Brattleboro, VT.: Stephen Greene Press, 1972.

_____. *Great American Lighthouses.* Washington, D.C.: The Preservation Press, 1989.

Marx, Robert. *Shipwrecks of the Western Hemisphere.* New York: David McKay Company, 1971.

McCormick, William Henry. *The Modern Book of Lighthouses, Lifeboats, and Lightships.* London: W. Heinemann, 1913.

McKee, Russell. *Great Lakes Country.* New York: Crowell, 1966.

Moe, Christine. *Lighthouses and Lightships.* Monticello, Ill.: 1979

Naush, John M. *Seamarks: Their History and Development.* London: Stanford Maritime, 1895.

Ratigan, William. *Great Lakes Shipwrecks and Survivals.* Grand Rapids, Mich.: Eerdmans Publishing, 1960.

Scheina, Robert L. "The Evolution of the Lighthouse Tower," *Lighthouses Then and Now* (supplement to the U.S. Coast Guard Commandant's Bulletin).

Snowe, Edward Rowe. *Famous Lighthouses of America.* New York: Dodd, Mead, 1955.

Tinney, James and Mary Burdette-Watkins. *Seaway Trail Lighthouses: An Illustrated Guide.* Oswego, N.Y.: Seaway Trail, Inc., 1989.

United States Coast Guard. *Historically Famous Lighthouses.* CG-232, 1986.

LIGHTHOUSE INDEX

FOR FURTHER INFORMATION
ON LIGHTHOUSES

Lighthouse Digest
P.O. Box 1690
Wells, ME 04090
(207) 646–0515

The *Digest* publishes an interesting monthly devoted to lighthouse news.

U.S. Lighthouse Society
244 Kearny Street, 5th Floor
San Francisco, CA 94108
(415) 362–7255

Members receive an interesting quarterly magazine about lighthouses, and the society conducts worldwide tours of lighthouses.

Great Lakes Lighthouse Keepers Association
P.O. Box 580
Allen Park, MI 48101

GLLKA publishes a quarterly journal for its members and hosts an annual meeting.

Lighthouse Preservation Society
P.O. Box 736
Rockport, MA 01966

LPS is known as an advocacy group and sponsors lighthouse conferences.

U.S. Coast Guard
Historian's Office G-CP/H
2100 2nd Street, SW
Washington, DC 20593

The Coast Guard History Office maintains operational records and historical materials related to the U.S. Coast Guard and its predecessor agencies.

National Archives
Record Group 26
Washington, DC 20408

Record Group 26 constitutes records of the Bureau of Lighthouses and its predecessors, 1789–1939, as well as U.S. Coast Guard records, 1828–1947, and cartographic and audiovisual materials, 1855–1963. These records are at the main archives building in Washington, DC. Some records, such as the individual lighthouse logs, are stored at the Suitland, Maryland, branch.

Ninth Coast Guard District
1240 East 9th Street
Cleveland, OH 44199–2060

The Ninth Coast Guard District is responsible for the operation and maintenance of the lighthouses on the Great Lakes. For permission to visit lighthouses not generally open to the public, contact the public affairs officer at this address.

The Great Lakes Historical Society
480 Main Street
Vermillion, OH 44089
(216) 967–3467

The Great Lakes Historical Society maintains an extensive museum and reference library on Great Lakes maritime history, including a wealth of information on lighthouses. It is well worth the time and effort to visit here.

Shore Village Museum
104 Limerock Street
Rockland, ME 04841

The Shore Village Museum has the most extensive collection of Fresnel lenses in America. A hands-on museum, it contains hundreds of lighthouse items.

National Park Service
Maritime Initiative
P.O. Box 37127
Washington, DC 20013-7127
(202) 343–9508

The Maritime Initiative is a database that contains the most accurate information available about American lighthouses.

National Park Service
Apostle Islands National Lakeshore
Bayfield, WI 54814
(715) 779–3397

One of the best collections of American lighthouses is now under the protection of the National Park Service in the Apostle Islands.

Door County Maritime Museum
c/o Door County Hardware
244 N. 3rd Avenue
Sturgeon Bay, WI 54235
(414) 743–8139

The Door County Maritime Museum is the best source of information on the fourteen lighthouses in Door County.

PHOTO INFORMATION

The pictures for this book were taken on Fuji 50 and Fuji 100 slide film. I'm sure other films would work just as well, but simplification is the only way I've survived as a professional travel photographer for the last few decades. I use only two Nikon Cameras (identical 8008s) with a small assortment of lenses. My tripod goes with me on every trip. When I was a young newspaper photographer, I thought tripods were for sissy photographers who were afraid to blur images. Now I think only fools don't use them. They ensure sharp pictures even at slow shutter speeds and give you time to compose when looking into the finder. A small Nikon flash SP-24 which fits into my camera bag, completes the equipment, except for polarizing and warming filters.

The cover photo of Split Rock Lighthouse was taken with a 35-mm lens on the Nikon 8008 at f 5.6, 1/30 of a second on Fuji 100 film, with a polarizing filter helping enrich the color. A few seconds after this picture was taken, clouds moved in, the sunlight disappeared, and the picture was gone. I used a tripod, not to permit a slow shutter speed, but rather to hold the exact composition while waiting for waves and sunlight.

For the picture of Lee Radzak with the Fresnel lens on page viii, a 24-mm wide-angle lens was used. I was standing on the catwalk outside the lantern room shooting through the glass. I waited until the Fresnel lens was not pointing directly into the camera so that the brilliance of the light beam would not flare in the lens. The key here was to shoot after sunset, with the fading daylight in the background. The camera was hand-held at 1/30 second on Fuji 100 film, with the lens at 2.8 to let in as much light as possible.

For the picture of the Fresnel lens on page iv at Dunkirk, New York, I used the tripod and an exposure of eight seconds at F.8 on my 500-mm Nikon telephoto lens. I was standing on the ground about 200 feet from the tower; but, by using a telephoto lens, I was able to create the feeling of being right beside it. It was about forty-five minutes after sunset; later the sky would go black instead of the night-time look of deep blue. I bracketed exposures—shooting one and two stops over and under as well as what I thought was the right setting. If it's worth shooting, I'm not stingy with film; besides, I see the film first when it comes back from processing and throw away the over and under stuff before anyone sees it. Editors think I'm expert with exposures, because they have never seen my waste basket. [Now I know.—Ed.]

The picture of the moon over the Frankfort light on page v was taken with the 500-mm telephoto on the tripod and an exposure of about twenty seconds. I looked at my watch right after I took this, and it was 10:10 at night, almost an hour after sunset; but I was shooting west into the last bit of afterglow, which made the sky orange.

For the picture of lightning behind the Grand Haven lights, the tripod made it possible. It was more than a half-hour past sunset, and I had been waiting for the lighthouse lights to come on. Then I saw the storm coming. I stopped the lens down to f.11 and started shooting twenty-second exposures, hoping the flash of lightning would come while the shutter was open—and it did. Then I packed up and got out of there before the storm blew in.

The pictures on pages 96, 81, and 52 of Sand Island, Cana Island, and Round Island were taken from a light plane. During my years of travel photography, I found that most small airports have a flying service where a plane can be rented and pilot hired by the hour, usually for under $100 for both. The more experienced pilots enjoy a photo flight, as it gives them a chance to practice their piloting skills a bit more than the usual trips. The Cessna 152 and 172 models are good, because the high wing allows you to shoot down without being blocked. The window also opens. (Try and hold the lens inside the slipstream of air.) I use my 33-135-mm telephoto for these air views and always try to keep the shutter speed up at 1/250 or 1/500. The latter is better. Good pilots have slowed the plane down for me; but to stay up in the air, we have to sweep by the lighthouse at seventy to eighty miles per hour, so fast shutter speeds are the only way to get sharp pictures. My standard shutter setting is 1/500 of a second.

I have found that air views look professional if I am down and leave out the horizon line at the top. Early morning or late afternoon are the best times for aerial photos, since the sun is low in the sky and creates shadows as the sunlight skims across the landscape.

During the day I use a polarizing filter when shooting in sunlight. It's easy to use—just rotate it around as you look through the camera and watch what happens. When the colors look their brightest, leave it there and shoot. All the sunlight shots were done with a polarizing filter. For overcast days and dusk photos (after the sun has gone below the horizon), I use a warming filter. My pick here is an 81C, which is a light brown-orange color. The photo of the Michigan City Pier Lights on page 89 needed even more color added. My maximum warming filter is a FL-D orange filter. I used it here because haze was blocking the color in the sky, making for a gray sunset. The orange filter brought the color back.

—BRUCE ROBERTS

ABOUT THE AUTHORS

BRUCE ROBERTS is a freelance photographer living in rural Virginia. He launched his wide-ranging career by working on newspapers in Tampa, Florida; Wilmington, Delaware; and Charlotte, North Carolina. Bruce served as director of photography and as senior photographer at *Southern Living* magazine for more than a decade. His award-winning photographs have also appeared in *Life, Sports Illustrated,* Time-Life Books, and many other magazines and books. Some of his photographs rest in the permanent collection of the Smithsonian Institution. Both the National and Georgia Nature conservancies have reprinted Bruce's nature photography.

RAY JONES is publisher of Country Roads Press, located in Castine, a small town on the coast of Maine. He began his writing career working as a reporter for weekly newspapers in Texas. He has served as an editor for Time-Life Books, as founding editor of *Albuquerque Living* magazine, and as a senior editor and writing coach at *Southern Living* magazine. Ray grew up in Macon, Georgia, where he was inspired by the writing of Ernest Hemingway and William Faulkner, and worked his way through college as a disc jockey.